NO TEST
NO TESTIMONY!

by Pamela Coston

Editor and Interior Designer: Tony Bradford

ISBN: 978-1-938950-43-8

Greater Is He Publishing

9824 E. Washington St.

Chagrin Falls, Ohio 44023

Phone: 216.288.9315

www.GreaterIsHePublishing.com

Dedications

I thank God for giving me the wisdom, and the courage, to write what has been written. I'm nothing without Him! To my priceless jewels Brandy and Heather, I thank God for lending you to me for a season. You've helped me to grow up and encouraged me when I wanted to give up. Thank you for my wonderful, precious, unique grandchildren, Fantazia, Jaron, Janaiah, Shailah, and Jaliaya. When I look at all of you I see greatness, so I'm releasing you into the capable hands of God. My love for you is immeasurable. When it's over for me on this side of the land, please don't worry about me! I will be awaiting your arrival on the other side.

I thank God for Elder Burton D. Clemons, first Lady Marion Gene Woo-Clemons, and my Tower of Prayer, Christ the King COGIC family. The endless words of encouragement and rebuke helped me to mature. My love for you hasn't diminished with time.

Thank you for your love and respect, and for the investment you made in my children and me.

The mentoring I received from the late Henry Wade Sr. is priceless. He lived what he taught, he said what he meant, and he meant what he said. I'm sending out a special thanks to Mother Mary Wade, Tanya and Karen Wade, Minister Jonathan and India Wade, and Pastor Henry Wade Jr. Being a part of the Frank Avenue COGIC family has blessed my life tremendously. Although God has changed the direction of my journey, my love for you will never change!

Auntie Barbara Hale, you said, "We will birth these messages together." Thank you for keeping your word. I thank God for (Jazzy) Jazzman Smith, Shelly Calhoun, and Cassandra Merolla. Your time and support has not been in vain. If I forgot to say I love you, forgive me. Ladies, I love you.

I dare not end this dedication without thanking Bishop William Smith and first lady Dr. Sherilyn Smith. Thank you for welcoming me into the Sanctuary of Praise family. Where I came from taught me how to appreciate where I am today. I'm honored to be a vital part of another amazing ministry that is lifting up the name of Jesus. In all that we do, *only what we do for Jesus Christ will last.*

CONTENTS

Chapter 1

Children Should be Seen and Heard!

Little Smiley, Your Name is_____

I have a lot to tell you, so here it is! I signed myself into the psychiatric ward at one of my favorite hospitals. The staff at the hospital knows me as the Cookie Lady. When the reason for my visit to the emergency room was disclosed, it shocked quite a few people. The unresolved issues in my life took me over the edge. I lost myself in other people. I'm not sure if I can live, or if I should just die. Why didn't God allow me to sleep on?

A little girl has lived inside of me for a long time. Daddy, I need to talk to you about a little girl named Little Smiley. She was abused by a so-called friend of her grandparents. The family members, who used and abused her, would have denied the abuse. She can't erase all of the filthy thoughts from her mind. The things that were done to her can't be undone. Little Smiley never forgot the name of the man who started off the abuse, nor the woman who wouldn't help her. The man's wife came down to the basement, but then she went back upstairs as if everything was all right. The woman was always drinking little brown bottles of beer. She seemed content in her sad world of deception!

The diabolical door of abuse also raped the mind of the child, who wasn't protected from her abusers. Little Smiley always felt alone, and she was ashamed of what was happening to her body. The people who were familiar to her have become the strangers she was taught to stay away from. The little girl is in a real bad place in her mind. She has been taught, "Children should be seen and not heard." No one rescued her from the horrible monsters who didn't go away. She couldn't wish them away. The little girl had convinced herself that she was just a nasty little girl. She believed the bad things that were happening to her were her fault.

Little Smiley told herself to be quiet, and she hoped the abuse would stop. When some of the horrific abuse stopped, it left the little girl quite traumatized. Could she recover from the abuse? She was afraid of both the light and the dark! She had cried too many tears in secret places. Now, the 42-year-old woman can't console or control the little girl, and she's about to snap. Her precious innocence was taken by people who had no right to do so. She lost her sense of security. No one protected her from the monsters, in or outside of her family.

The woman can't tell anyone about the dirty, dark secrets, but the little girl is tired of hiding. She has anger issues; the pain of the past is coming out. A war has erupted between the woman and the little girl. The woman is struggling to deal with the dark issues buried inside of her. Unwanted thoughts of suicide are invading her mind as she struggles to hold on. Suicide isn't an option, for it won't heal her heartache. The woman has prayed for God to take her home, to be with him. The world has become a place she doesn't want to be.

Why didn't He take the woman home; didn't He want her? Who can erase the painful memories of the woman's past? She hid within the little girl, so no one could see her for who she was. She gained a lot of weight to cover up her shapely body, which has attracted the wrong attention. The woman can't hide the excess weight from men who are attracted to abundantly blessed women. The cover-up didn't work. Now she's stuck with excess weight she has to get rid of.

The woman also tried to hide behind her unique sense of humor. Hiding out is what she does best. She doesn't have a social life; she's too busy fixing issues for other people because she can't fix her own. The little girl keeps telling the woman, "You can't trust anyone, especially men." When the abusers were done with the nasty little girl, they tossed her aside like a piece of trash. She can no longer protect the woman. Now it's time for the woman to be heard, healed, and set free. Pain and fear have crippled her ability to live the life that God had ordained for her. It's time for her to keep Romans 8:37* in her heart: "Yet in all things we are more than conquerors through Him who loved us."

The little girl's grandparents called her Smiley because she smiled all the time. The smiles were a cover-up to hide the tears that fell in secret places. If her grandparents or her guardians, Eddie and Barbara, had found out about the abuse, it would have devastated them. Her uncle Eddie and her grandfather may have gone to jail after dealing with her abusers. A shift of goodness is about to change the course of the angry woman's life. The life God has planned for her is better than what she has settled for.

The drama the woman endured isn't like the movie, "The Wizard of Oz." There's no yellow brick road. There's no tin man, cowardly lion, or a little cute dog to travel down the road of life with her. The only scarecrow who wants to travel with the woman is the enemy of her soul. The woman isn't off to see the "Wonderful Wizard of Oz," and her name isn't Dorothy. It's going to take more than three clicks of any ruby red slippers to get back home. In "The

Wizard of Oz," the cowardly lion found his courage within himself. How could the scarecrow say, "If I only had a brain," if he didn't have a brain? The tin man found the heart he was looking for within himself! I ate the meat and spit out the bones when using bits and pieces of the movie, "The Wizard of Oz."

I'm about to introduce someone to the little girl before she goes. She's a beautiful African Queen and is the proud mother of two precious jewels named Brandy and Heather. Motherhood has been difficult for her, but she refused to give up on her children when she wanted to give up on herself. The woman is truly loved by her daughters, her church family, and some of her biological family. I'm not talking about the people who inspired the message, "How low are you willing to go?"

Little Smiley, you're the little girl Pam hid behind; now, it's time for Ms. Pamela Jean Coston to come out. She's the apple of God's eye. She's fighting to become who she's supposed to be. She is as sweet as honey, but the lioness in her isn't to be messed with. She's using the tailor-made ministry God has loaned her to glorify Him, and Him alone.

God has allowed me to share one of the most excruciating seasons of my life. I spent the majority of my life blaming Him, the people who didn't help me, and myself. If God had not been there for me, I would not have made it this far! What I suffered through is happening to someone else as I'm writing this. Our abused children are afraid of the light and the dark. Parents, pay close attention to your child. If your child shies away from someone, please don't ignore the warning signs. The signs are there for a reason!

Abuse can be found in any home, and the abusers may be closer than you think. I hope this message will snatch someone from the darkness of their past. It's time to unmask all of the dark secrets and monsters of our past. I pray for people who are in a bad place in their heart or their mind. I pray for injured people who are ready to give up on life. Please hold on. I send the word of God to encourage you right now. Trust me; Jesus is the solution for all of your problems. Please don't give up on yourself! You're worth the price Jesus paid for you, so get up and live.

I'm no longer worried about my reputation, so read on. The week that I spent in the psychiatric ward was a blessing in disguise. I met other hurting people who confessed why they were in and out of the psychiatric ward. The visitors who showed up looked as if they were ready to go before the visit even started. I didn't want anyone to know where I was. I was trying to deal with the issues, which had taken me to a secret passage in my mind. Fear, shame and anger will cause hurting people to back away from help that's provided for them. When I came to myself, it occurred to me that I was truly blessed. God and my loved ones had not thrown me away; I had thrown myself away! I tried to fix the issues in my life on my own! In the wise words of Dr. Phil, "How's that working for you?" Well, it didn't work for me. That's why I ended up in the psychiatric ward. After I signed myself out of the psychiatric ward, someone invited me to a church luncheon. In the middle of a conversation, someone said, "Sister Pam, I heard you were in the hospital. Why were you in the hospital? When I gave them the truth, it didn't go over well. The woman said, "Saints of God don't have nervous breakdowns." Another seasoned saint of God came to my rescue. My hero said, "I beg your pardon; saints of God have problems like anyone else!"

I was shocked when other women came to my rescue. They didn't rebuke me; they encouraged me. The enemy tried to shame me back into hiding. I was hurt by what the judgmental person said. I loved her, but I refused to receive what she said about me. Look for the message, *"I don't receive that."* Listen, after the open rebuke, I had to hold my head up, even when I felt like holding it down.

I refuse to cover up, or shut up, about the issues that are happening in and outside of our churches. No one can testify about what God has done for me like I can. He has given so much of Himself to me that I am truly honored to give myself back to Him. In the midst of my tears, there was joy and doses of laughter. As we grow up in God, growing pains at any age are very painful. The enemy wants us to focus on our pain until it consumes us, one issue at a time.

Some people are going to say I've shared too much. I'm okay with that! It hasn't been easy for me to share the most difficult issues of my life. I won't apologize for God using me! I thought He had set me free from the little girl. I thought she was gone. When my dearest friend/mentor Mother Leona Derrington-Butler and I were talking on the phone, the issues of my past molestations came up. When the pain, shame, anger, and fear surfaced, it got ugly. I began to cry, moan, wail, and scream as Mother Butler prayed for me. I knew the little girl was gone when she said, "You're safe!" For the first time in my life, I knew everything was going to be all right. The little girl that was cast out of me in 2005 tried to come back, but I didn't allow her to come back into my blessed life. My guardians taught me children should stay out of grown-up people's business. God confirmed this when He spoke something so sweet into my spirit. I'll tell you what He told me after you read the poem He inspired me to write.

Little Smiley, my daddy holds my future
He holds my trembling hand
He's my peace that passes understanding
When there are things I don't understand
Little Smiley, it's time to let you go
It's time for Pam to come forth and grow
I thank God for the beautiful sunshine
As well as the refreshing rain
What I've learned isn't wasted
None of my trials have been in vain
Daddy, now I can see
I'm becoming who you ordained me to be
Pam's no longer dead and buried
Her wonderful daddy has set her free

Wasn't that a sweet poem from my daddy? Okay, this is what He told me that encouraged me to keep the little girl out of my life: "I would not have given a husband to a little girl." I'm no longer afraid to walk the steps God has ordered for me. He's able to walk with me, or carry me when I'm not able to walk on my own. Guess what–the blessings of the Lord God Almighty are for Pam, not the little girl!

Unless otherwise stated, Biblical references are from the KJV.

It Always Rains Before a Rainbow!

By Miss Fantazia Coston, July 23, 2012

As I was sitting in school, I remember we had to write a deep poem in my English class. I chose to write mine on a rather heated subject, suicide. We could choose to write the poem anonymously, and I took that option. When my teacher got done reading my poem I could tell by his face that he probably thought, *how could a fourteen-year-old girl know so much about life? She hasn't even been on this earth for much more than a decade.* It's crazy, but I feel like there's a grown woman inside my teenaged body. I had to grow up too fast!

My mother was addicted to drugs during most of my childhood. I took on the role as the "second mother" to my brother and sister. My mother wasn't around. On February 27, my mother will have been clean for six years. I'm so proud of her! We went from living in my mother's best friend's basement to moving to Cleveland with almost nothing. We moved from a small apartment into a really nice house. We have two cars. My mother has a good job that pays her really well. She is now working on her bachelor's degree.

I could sit here and write about every bad thing that has happened to me, and who I could blame. I'd rather tell you where I came from and how I got here. Everyone has a past, so why should we sit around and dwell on it? Why not focus on the present and the future? Whether you like it or not, life goes on, with or without you. No matter how bad people have treated you, you must find it in your heart to forgive them! If you don't forgive them, you will end up miserable. It always rains before a rainbow! Basically, the darkness will come before it gets light. Everything does happen for a reason.

Gone Fishing!

This message was inspired by my grandparents, Albert and Estella Davis. Just sit back and relax. Let me take you on a few of our fishing adventures. My grandparents and I loved to fish. Each of us had our favorite place to fish. My favorite spot had a playground. I was allowed to play on the playground while they fished on the shore. When my grandparents wanted to fish on the lake, they rented a boat. The boat was equipped with a motor and a set of oars. Before we began our fishing adventure, we had to put on life preservers. After the boat was loaded, it was time to catch some fish.

The pre-fishing adventure, which started the night before, grossed me out. When one of my grandparents dug a hole in the front yard, the other one shined a flashlight in the hole. If any of the disgusting creeping night crawlers couldn't get away, they ended up in a container. If you don't mind, I'm leaving the bait topic alone for a moment. I'll return to that when I'm able to stomach it.

My grandparents looked like true athletes as they rowed the boat. They deserved a ten for their rowing abilities. When we arrived at our favorite spot, the anchor was dropped. The fishing gear and the bait were pulled out. The hooks were baited with the slow night crawlers that didn't get away! I could fish all day if I didn't have to bait the hook. At home, I ran countless errands for my grandparents. I soaked their tired feet. I cut toenails that weren't easy to cut. Was I being trained to step out of my comfort zone? Don't you think my grandparents should have baited the hooks for me? I do!

Why didn't we use the artificial bait in the tackle box? It was nestled among the bobbers, hooks, pliers, floaters, and the fishing line. The artificial bait wasn't creepy; it didn't crawl away; it just laid there! My grandparents said, "The artificial bait is used to catch a certain type of fish." As a child, I had to accept what was said to me as the truth. The cliché, *Children should be seen and not heard,* no longer works for me. I'm not a child anymore; what I need to say will be heard. Are you ready to hear about our unsafe lunchtime on the boat? It was almost as disgusting as the bait issue.

My grandmother always packed our lunch before our fishing adventures. The lunch was packed in a brown paper bag and placed under the seat of the boat. After we had fished for a while, it was time to eat. Grandma secured her pole, leaned over the side of the boat, and swished her hands in the water. After she had dried her hands with an old dingy rag, she divided up the sun-warmed lunch. My grandfather and I did what she did so we could eat our lunch.

There are a few sanitation and safety issues which need to be addressed: (1) We could have fallen overboard as we were swishing our hands in the lake water. (2) There wasn't any soap, sanitizer, or clean rags on the boat. (3) It's a miracle none of us got sick eating sun-warmed food with unsanitary hands. Lunchtime is over; it's time to fish for a meal, which could have been purchased. We often went home with nothing but a sun tan. It didn't matter if we didn't catch any fish. We loved to fish. I didn't value the time I spent with my grandparents, but now I can treasure our precious moments and share them with you.

As Christians, we are told to be "fishers of men." Too many so-called artificial fishermen are using the wrong bait to catch people. The people who are caught with the wrong bait may jump back into the world. Did the artificial fishermen comment strike a nerve? Do you need a moment to do a spiritual check? Go ahead, I've already done mine. The spirit of humility allows me to see myself. I'm not foolish enough to act as if "I'm all that." Let me make it plain: God is the only "I am that I am." He is all that and so much more!

Whenever my grandparents caught a fish, they examined it as they were removing the hook from its mouth. If the fishhook was embedded in the mouth of the fish, out came the pliers from the tackle box. After the hook was skillfully removed, the fish was either kept or, if it wasn't the right kind or size, thrown back into the water. Is this how we treat people who don't measure up to our standards as fishers of men? Why do we throw them back into the world they tried to escape from? Shame on us, if we mistreat anyone in the name of God!

My grandparents were experienced fishermen. They knew what bait to use in order to catch a certain fish. Are we using the methods that have worked down through the years? We must use real weapons to fight a real enemy! We must arm ourselves with the right gear so we can reach those who are lost. If we don't catch the people who are being drawn by God, there may be hell to pay! We are told to be *fishers* of men, not *cleaners* of men! God is the only one who's qualified to clean us up! If we use the right bait, we'll catch men, women, boys, and girls. Then and only then, we will earn the right to be called, "fishers of men!"

I Also Have a Dream!

When I was a teenager, I heard an unforgettable speech that was delivered by the late, great, Dr. Martin Luther King, Jr. When he delivered his "I Have a Dream" speech, it impacted the nation. He became a target of those who feared him. No one has been able to recite the "I Have a Dream" speech like Dr. King. You could hear the compassion and the concern he had for the entire world. The dreamer was silenced too soon, but his dreams will live on. We will not let the dreams of the courageous dreamer die!

Dr King told us to work hard to get where we're going. He said, "We will make it to the Promised Land." Would he be pleased with the progress that we as a people have made? Will our passion for life become a legacy of greatness after we are gone? If we give in to the pressures of life, we will move backwards, not forward! We've come too far to let anyone or anything distract us from our destiny. This is the appropriate time to use a quote from Reverend Jessie Jackson: "We must keep hope alive." If we allow our hope to die, we will die! This message is about dreams, so here are a few of my dreams. My hope is they will inspire you to dream your own dreams!

I dream that my life will glorify God; after all, He did give His only begotten son, Jesus Christ, for me. I'm ready to live my richly blessed, abundant life without limits or regrets.

I dream that we will love our children as God loves them! The diabolical cycle of child abuse must be destroyed. It has stolen the lives and innocence of our priceless jewels.

I dream that, as women, we will know giving birth to a child doesn't necessarily qualify us as a mother. Some of the greatest mothers are the women who didn't give birth. These women have stepped in to take care of babies who needed them. I chose to be a good mother to Brandy and Heather, even if their fathers chose not to be good fathers.

I dream that real men will become positive role models for the children they fathered. Donating sperm doesn't make you a father. If you are not willing to take responsibilities for your actions, keep your lust under control. We don't need any more negligent, irresponsible sperm donors!

I dream that no addiction will hold us hostage. This may sound like an impossible dream, but I'm not taking it off my list of dreams.

I dream that our children will feel safe, in or outside of their homes. You can understand why this is so important to me after reading "Little Smiley, your name is ___."

I dream that real men will be proud to take charge in their relationship. Don't put a woman in a position where she is forced to wear the pants! A man who refuses to wear the pants, tailor-made for him, turns off most women.

I dream that, as women, we will realize the hands of the Master Artist have crafted us. God made us from a man, but we don't need a man to validate or complete us. I'm not part of an equation; I am a whole woman.

I dream that my beautiful skin color is no longer seen as a stereotypical issue. My beautiful flavor has added something unique to this sin-infested world. My inner beauty won't fade as time ticks on. No form of makeup can cover up inner ugliness.

I dream that the vision of where God is taking me will remain clear when my natural vision begins to change. My focus is on Him. I can't afford to lose sight of God. He has been too good to me.

I dream that my ears will always be open to the needs of others. Excuse me for a minute. I just heard a mother cursing at the precious jewels God loaned her. Was it meant for me to hear the stressed-out mother? Instead of judging her, I must pray for her. I don't know what she's going through, but God does!

I dream that the size of a person's heart will become more important than the size of their body. When I weighed over 350 lbs., the food police told me what I didn't need to eat. Wow, didn't they think I was aware of my weight problem? While they were on their post, monitoring the food I was eating, they failed to see what was eating at me!

I dream that, as women, we will stop allowing men to sample our goodies until they've had enough of what we have to offer. Women, we must stop seeing only what we want to see! It's time to show Mr. Sampler we are no longer on anyone's menu!

I dream that my children and my grandchildren will live a life that glorifies God. I pray that they will love Him and one another unconditionally.

We may or may not have the same dreams. Just dare to dream! My final dream can be found in St. Matthew 25:21. "His Lord said unto him, 'Well done thou good and faithful servant; thou hast been faithful over a few things, I will make thee ruler over many things: enter into the joy of thy Lord.'" Dream on, dreamers, dream on!

Chapter 2

No Test, no Testimony

Weak in her Body,
Strong in her faith!

I've read stories about the woman who had an issue of blood. Each account of the courageous woman can be found in Matthew 9:20-22, Mark 5:25-34, and Luke 8:43-48. Now, according to each of the stories, the afflicted woman spent all of her money on doctors. They couldn't help her, so she continued to suffer with the condition for over twelve years. Her body grew weaker, but her faith still remained strong.

The stranger, who was passing through the city, was no stranger to the needs of His people. Hope rose up in the woman when she heard Jesus Christ had arrived at her city. She had to reach Him; she needed to touch the hem of His garment. Jesus was about to be touched in an unusual way. The healing virtue in His body was about to flow into the body of the afflicted woman.

The woman was considered unclean because of her condition. She wasn't allowed to touch anyone. If the doctors weren't allowed to touch her, how did they treat her? Did they just suggest various things that might help her? Was her money considered clean or unclean? Feel free to answer any of my questions. The doctors who didn't help the woman didn't have a problem helping themselves to her clean or unclean money!

Her season of affliction was about to come to an end. She was about to press through a crowd of people who didn't want her to touch them. She had to reach the One who did want her to touch Him. When she reached Jesus, there was no turning back. She had to find the strength and the courage to reach up and touch the hem of His garment. She kept her focus on what she needed from Jesus. It was her day for a miracle.

While I was writing this, my mind reflected back to my daughter Brandy. With each pregnancy, she faced excruciating emotional and physical pain. Brandy chose to raise her children even if the father of her children didn't help her. I'm proud of you, Brandy. I love you and your beautiful jewels Fantazia, Jaron, and Janaiah. When I asked her if what she went through was worth it, she quickly said, "Yes, Mommy, it was worth it."

Will our faith see us through the storms of life, or will doubt choke out our faith, like a stillborn baby? The woman didn't allow fear or doubt to rob her of her miracle. When she touched the hem of Jesus' garment, the flow of blood instantly stopped. When Jesus asked who touched Him, the disciples didn't understand what He was asking them! As they looked around at the number of people in the crowd, they couldn't discern who had touched Him. Jesus wasn't talking about a physical touch. The healing virtue, which came out of Jesus, went into the body of the afflicted woman and totally healed her.

When the healed woman confessed what she did, Jesus didn't rebuke her. He praised her for her courage and remarkable faith. He told her to go in peace. Her faith in Jesus opened up the door for her to be healed and made whole. The peace she received was an added bonus for her touching the hem of Jesus' garment. We can still touch Jesus with our faith. Whatever we need is in the name and the precious blood of Jesus Christ!

Homeless, but not Godless!

How do we feel about homeless people? Are they dirty eyesores which shouldn't be seen or heard? Homeless people are everywhere–they won't be ignored! How dare we forget the cliché, "but there by the grace of God, go I." Many people who celebrate their climb up the ladder of success will come crashing down in an instant. Here's a golden nugget from Grandma Estella: "Every bird that flies high has to come down for a drink of water." The people who are exalted in their selfish minds may be one step away from becoming homeless. Here's another rich nugget: "Be careful of the people you trample on your way up, for you may meet them on your way down." If you haven't changed the way you feel about homeless people, read on, or stop reading!

Don't get me wrong; there are honest people who have worked hard to get where they are. They know their success can change in an instant. They don't announce their good deeds. They will reap the goodness they have sown. Compassionate people will reap much compassion. Merciless people won't receive mercy when they need it the most!

Allow me to introduce you to some M&M people. These phony, superficial people are members of the "Me and Mine club." Their focus is only on themselves and their loved ones. They're not about to waste their precious time, love, money, or concern on people who are outside of their pitiful circle. They open up their refrigerator, but they don't want what's in there. They decide to order some takeout food. Will the leftovers be shoved into the packed refrigerator, or will they be thrown away? The M&M club members wear their tailor-made success like a glove. If they lose everything, they become invisible like the people they refused to see or help!

Now that you've become homeless, your past membership in the M&M club won't secure you a VIP spot in a soup line. You can't call in to make a reservation at a homeless shelter with upgrades. Now that you're homeless, will any of the members of the M&M club reach out to help you? Now that the not-so-fresh-smelling shoes are on your feet, how does it feel to be homeless? This issue is difficult to write about. It's very close to my heart. My heart goes out to any person who's in a bad place, regardless of how they got there.

My daughters and I moved from the projects of Barberton into our first house. Our dream house turned into a nightmare when our landlords turned into slumlords. Their lies slowly drew us into their web of deceit. Within a few weeks, someone came out to read the water meter. When we received our first water bill, it was over fourteen hundred dollars. Another meter reader came out to re-read the meter. She said a water leak might explain such a high meter reading.

When a meeting at the water department was set up, the landlords/slumlords didn't show up. I explained my side of the past-due water bill issue. The officials expressed their anger and their disgust for landlords/slumlords. The bottom line didn't disappear. The past-due bill had to be paid. Now what! My daughters and I couldn't pay the bill. The slumlords refused to pay the bill.

God, please help us. They're turning the water off. How are we going to live in a waterless house? In a short time, we developed a system of keeping the house and ourselves clean. Nobody knew our water was off until they needed to use the bathroom. We collected water from our neighbor and friends until the weather got too bad. Yes, they turned our water off in the middle of winter. Living in the waterless house took a toll on my body. During my illness, I had to make a painful decision.

I took my daughters to live with John and Lessie Kirkland-Smith. I went to stay at a shelter. When the intake worker asked me what caused us to become homeless, I started to cry. I kept thinking about my daughters. As long as they were safe, I could stay at the shelter. I was thankful for a place to stay, but I was angry about the whole water bill issue.

When the other homeless women and I went over to the dining room, I seldom ate. I didn't want to talk to anyone, nor did I want anyone to talk to me. I tried to tune out the discussions that were going on around me. I held onto my salty attitude until I reached out to God. He's the only one who's able to help us when we're in trouble. I began to rebuke the "Oh, woe is me" spirit. Enough of the "it's all about me" drama. I had glorified the enemy of my soul for too long.

We had to sign up for a bed every day. After we took our showers, we could relax until the lights were turned off. Some of the ladies began to come into our dorm room to talk. They began to confess how they became homeless. Their horrific stories of abuse made our waterless home drama seem trivial. We didn't have a monopoly on pain or drama! God brought all of us together for a season. We were homeless, but we weren't Godless! One of the young ladies used to stop and look around whenever we went outside. She later told us she was hiding from her abuser.

The ladies began to talk about their addictions that led them to commit criminal acts. They talked about prostitution, stealing, drugs, and abuse. With each confession their walls of shame, fear, anger, and disappointment began to crumble. It was awesome to see the transformations of some of the women. We knew we were safe from the storms that were waiting for us outside of the shelter. The shelter was set up as a temporary haven. It wasn't set up to become a permanent home for the homeless!

The number of homeless people is increasing daily. How many of them have given up on life and themselves? Can any person use their homelessness as a stepping-stone instead of a stumbling block? Yes they can. I'm stepping over my stumbling blocks to help other people.

Time to shut the pity party down! I'm about to make the best of the storm that has come into our lives. I'm crying out for God to help us. Every filthy negative spirit had to go! I wasted so much time being embarrassed and angry at the slumlords. I had to believe God was about to turn things around for us. A peace rose up within me, which took me past my understanding.

I almost forgot to tell you about the people who said, "Homeless people choose to be homeless." The inhumane statement shocked me and left me speechless. In all of the conversations the ladies and I had, none of us woke up and said, "Hey, this is a wonderful day to become homeless." When God used me to speak at one of our combined church services, I declared we're valuable human beings, we're not invisible, and we are not Godless! When I changed my not-so-sweet attitude, situations began to change! I stopped crying and began to smile as I went through my test. I began to thank God for the services provided for us as homeless people.

The ladies and I started to have bible study in our dorm room. They tried not to cuss in front of me, but they didn't sugar coat what they were dealing with. As we shared our past regrets, we bonded together, one confession at a time. Here's a quote from my dear friend Lessie, for it fits this message like a glove: "I can't hear what you're saying unless I know you care." The women knew God and I loved them. They weren't judged by how they looked or how they acted.

God blessed me to find out about a job opening at Walmart. As soon as I filled out the application, I was interviewed and hired on the spot. If I had to work late, a staff member at the shelter would let me in. They made sure I had eaten and had a clean bed to sleep in. When it was time to leave the shelter, I said goodbye to the wonderful staff. They went beyond their job description to serve us. They were kind, compassionate, and patient, but they knew how to shut all of the confusion down. It was hard to say goodbye to the ladies I had grown to love and respect. They humbled me and allowed me to see I was blessed in spite of the waterless home drama. I hope they will never forget they're somebody in God. I pray they'll seek God for what they need. After I left the safe haven of the shelter, I went to pick up my daughters. I had to confront what I needed to conquer!

My anger, pride, frustration, and health issues took me where I needed to be for the moment. My faith in God took us back to the waterless house for a short time. There's a cliché which says, "You won't miss your water until your well runs dry." That's true, but "we didn't miss our water until the pipes ran dry." When we moved into the next house, it didn't come with a past-due water bill!

I can't close this message without sharing what my gifted, unique friend Pastor Gregory Jordan said while he was running a revival at Christ the King COGIC. As he began to minister he said, "I thank God for the things I don't have to pray about!" Someone asked him to repeat what he had flung into the atmosphere. While some of us were rejoicing, he repeated the profound statement. If we pray about the issues we're facing, we won't get caught up with the issues God has already worked out! If we focus on the goodness of the Lord, bountiful blessings will explode into every area of our lives.

I refuse to lie to you and say that my daughters and I enjoyed any of the storms that came into our lives. I can tell you that we had to trust God, even when it seemed as if He didn't care about what we were going through. He assured us that He was in control of our out of control issues! When I got out of the way and trusted Him, He took care of our needs and us. He was waiting for me to surrender everything into His capable hands.

No Test, No Testimony!

When I heard the words, "no test, no testimony," I knew a test was on the way! If we don't pass our test, we won't have anything to testify! As I was writing this message, the Holy Ghost gave me Romans 4:18-21. Let me share verse 20-21 with you: (20) "He staggered not at the promises of God through unbelief; but was strong in faith, giving glory to God. (21) And being fully persuaded that what He had promised, He was able to perform."

The angels of God told Abraham that his wife Sarah was going to bear him a son. This seemed impossible considering how old they were at the time of the promise. Is there anything too hard for God? No, there's nothing too hard for Him. He kept the promise He made to Abraham and Sarah. They named their baby boy Isaac. Abraham was about to be tested in a way beyond his comprehension. The test would confirm that he truly trusted God. He told him to offer up Isaac, his son of promise, as a sacrifice. Was he willing to do what God asked him to do? Just as he was about to offer up Isaac, the angel of the Lord told him not to harm his son. He sacrificed the ram caught in the bush. Abraham didn't stagger at the promises of God. He truly trusted Him, even when he didn't understand Him.

When someone staggers for whatever reason, they might fall down. If we stagger at the promises of God, we may fall into the traps set by the enemy of our soul. When it seems as if our prayers won't be answered, what should we do? Be still, and know God is still in control. I'm about to free myself. I had to take some of my tests over and over again until I passed them. When we pass a test, though, we can't get too comfortable, for another one is on the way!

Since I failed to renew my driver's license in time, I had to take the entire test over again. I passed the written test with flying colors. I couldn't believe I flunked the maneuverability test. I knocked one of the cones over. When I retook the test, the cones were left intact. They didn't issue my driver's license until I passed the part of the test I had flunked. The challenges of life will intensify as we reach new levels in God. When we study His word, it will prepare us for upcoming tests. We must trust God when we're going through new ones. We must keep our focus on Him, not the test. The hardest part of a testimony is the test. If we don't pass our test, there will be no testimony!

Business as Usual!

When "The Passion of the Christ" was released, people flocked to the theaters to view the movie. Some members of the audience were interviewed after it was over. Some of them said they were moved to tears; others said the violence was too graphic. Mr. Mel Gibson, the producer of the movie, called attention to what Jesus Christ did for us.

Critics said that "The Passion of the Christ" was controversial. We'll leave the critics alone with their words of criticism. When I was given a DVD of the movie as a Christmas present, I didn't watch it right away. Nothing could have prepared me for what I was about to see. I was about to be taken on an emotional roller coaster. I tried to convince myself these were just actors playing various roles. Each of the gifted, talented actors played their roles with such passion. They made "The Passion of the Christ" real for both believers and non-believers. It was hard to watch the scenes where the actor who portrayed Jesus was violently beaten and tortured.

Let me back up for a moment. The scene where Judas betrayed Jesus was also difficult to watch. He couldn't erase the pain he saw in Jesus' eyes. He wasn't about to live a business-as-usual life after he betrayed Jesus. He sealed his fate by hanging himself. Judas left a legacy of betrayal behind.

Jesus never cried out against those who shouted for him to be crucified. He didn't call out for the torture to stop. He was betrayed and abandoned by those who claimed to love Him. He suffered for the people who loved Him or hated Him. Jesus Christ suffered for those who did or didn't believe. He was the Son of God. Oh my God, please help me, for the struggle to birth this message is excruciating. The labor pains have intensified. It's time to push; the baby's on the way.

Some of the scenes of "The Passion of the Christ" were too painful to watch. The price Jesus paid for us can never be repaid. He came to this sin-sick, infested world as a humble servant. He came to fulfill the purpose that had been lost. He didn't enter the world as a high official. He came to save us from the enemy of our soul. Jesus faced a trial that was fixed against Him. He was found guilty as charged and sentenced to be crucified. The notorious criminal, Barabbas, was released to commit other crimes! Jesus came to carry our sin and diseases on an old rugged cross.

I tried to wrap my mind around what happened over two thousand years ago. We can apply the excruciating stripes Jesus took for us to every area of our lives. Jesus took the lashes from the guards, who ripped his back to shreds. As the camera scanned the crowd, it showed those who enjoyed what Jesus chose to endure. It also showed the people who were devastated by what they saw. The actress who played the role of Mary, the mother of Jesus, captivated my heart. The movie captured the love a true mother has for her child. Jesus was her Son and her Savior, wrapped up together in one totally awesome temple.

Mary couldn't stop the horrific drama she had to witness. She knew her son/Savior Jesus was about to fulfill His destiny. Her piercing eyes said what she couldn't say. Her heart was being ripped apart as the back of Jesus was being ripped to shreds. He didn't cry out as the cross tore into His mutilated flesh; He took the excruciating steps toward His destiny.

A few of the scenes in "The Passion of the Christ" made me angry. I'm not sure I will be able to turn my other cheek if someone slaps me. Could I wipe the spit off my beautifully aged face? Could I just walk away from the person who spit on me or slapped me? Amen for those of you that will pass the "slap you, spit-in-your face" test. You may need to pray for me for real; amen for the truth!

God ordained the people who played parts in the life, death, and resurrection of Jesus. When Jesus Christ declared, "It is finished," His assignment had been completed. His final declaration left an impact on the entire world. When He died, however, that wasn't the end of the story. He didn't stay dead. I can't get into what happened on that marvelous third day. Rejoice with me as I move on to the next thought. The movie, "The Passion of the Christ," stirred up a range of emotions. As the images of the movie began to fade, it became business as usual. What do I mean by the term, "business as usual?"

If we're judged by the color of our skin instead of the contents of our character, it's "business as usual." If we're judged by what we have or don't have instead of who we are, it's "business as usual." If "The Passion of the Christ" is seen as just another controversial movie, it's still "business as usual."

On the first day of March in 2005, something occurred that confirmed this message. My friend Monique, her son Zavion, and I set out to help someone who had a special need. It's nothing to brag about, for it's listed in the bible as reasonable service. Just as we finished our shopping, the weather got really bad. All of a sudden, the car began to slide out of control. Zavion yelled, "Sweet baby Jesus!" I cried out, "Oh sweet Jesus!" and Monique didn't say anything.

God kept us from going over the side of the cliff, and then He kept the oncoming traffic from hitting us. When the near-death incident was over, Monique said, "I saw us going over the side of the cliff." God didn't allow what she saw to come to pass. After our near-death experience, we laughed and talked and tried to make light of what happened to us. We thanked God and moved on with our "business as usual lives."

A series of tragedies brought our neighborhood together for a season. A young man was murdered as he confronted people who crashed his girlfriend's birthday party. Only God can heal her as she mourns the death of the boyfriend, who will never celebrate another birthday.

A little boy's life was snatched by cowards who were shooting at one another. Their filthy spirit of hate drove them to murder an innocent boy. Their cowardly act changed the destiny of his short life. He didn't deserve to become a victim of hate. His lifeless body had to be embalmed, dressed, and viewed by loved ones who were forced to face something they didn't ask for. This is for the people who are looking for revenge: If you don't get rid of the hate that is festering inside of you, it will destroy you.

How many of you still have a VCR? A movie can be rewound so it can be restarted. If you have the new digital program, you can start a program over. You can't press a remote to restart the life of the person you murdered! From the tragedies to our near-death experience, did any of us have time to get right with God? If you haven't repented for all of your sins, please do it now! Don't miss another opportunity to get right. Death has the ability to sneak up on us! Our soul will end up in heaven or hell. When we get right, we will get rid of our "business as usual attitude!"

Hold on and Don't Let Go!

I'll start this message off with the lyrics of a sweet song: "I shall never let go of His hands; He has done so much for me, I shall never let go of His hands." These words can minister to you if you are, or even if you are not, in the will of God. Don't you dare give up! Please, hold on. Your help is on the way. Are you facing a trial that has dropped you to your knees? Has the pain caused you to soak your pillow with tears? You may not be able to cry–the pain may cause you to moan and groan. Welcome to the "Hold-on-and-don't-let-go club." Jesus Christ paid your membership fee a long time ago.

Have you ever felt as if your heart was being ripped apart? The death of a loved one or the death of a relationship can take you to a bad place. The death of a marriage can rip your life apart. How can you erase the words, "What God has joined together let no man put asunder" from your mind? I can tell you from experience that there is life after a divorce!

The trials that we face will show us what we're made of. As we face our trials, let us remember the lyrics, "I shall never let go of His hands; help us to hold on to God's unchanging hand. He said that the things that caused me to break, would cause me to bend, and then I would no longer bend." Those wonderful words of encouragement gave me the strength to hold onto His powerful but gentle hands.

When our trials take us past our understanding, hold on to Proverbs 3: 5-6, "Trust in the Lord with all thine heart, and lean not on your own understanding. In all your ways acknowledge Him, and He shall direct your paths." If we put our trust in other people and fail to trust God, we will be disappointed. He will never make a promise that He won't keep.

The mothers in St Matthew 2:18 faced a tragedy which tore their hearts and their lives apart. "A voice was heard in Ramah, lamentations, weeping, and great mourning, Rachel weeping for her children, refusing to be comforted, because they were no more."

How could the grieving mothers hold onto God's hand as their babies were slaughtered in front of their eyes? When my mentor friend Mother Delores Moorer lost her son Donnie, I didn't tell her that I knew how she felt. Even if she and I were facing the same trial, we would not feel the same way! I truly don't want to know how it feels to lose either of my daughters. I'm being honest and real. Mother Moorer did hold onto God's hand during the most painful time of her life.

My grandmother Estella was full of wisdom. Her rich nuggets have blessed me down through the years. She came up with stories to fit any occasion. I'm honoring her memory by passing down her legacy of wisdom and greatness. Now, God has given me my own unique stories and rich nuggets to pass down! Well, get ready–it's story time. This short story was inspired by my beautiful, unusual granddaughter, Fantazia. She's three years old and she's quite thick for her age.

When I decided to walk to the neighborhood drug store, I took her with me. Big mistake! I'm about six feet tall. Can you imagine her trying to keep up with me? I tried to carry her for a while, another big mistake! I allowed Fantazia to walk at her snail pace. Her slow-as-corrosion pace got on my impatient nerves.

I finally grabbed her thick little hands to hurry her up. On the way back home, Fantazia made an ugly face and let go of my hand. She was tired of trying to keep up with my long-legged pace. I allowed her to enjoy her freedom. She began to sing and play. All of a sudden she started screaming, "A bug, Hanma, a bug!" Fantazia grabbed my hand and held onto it until we reached the apartment. I didn't run to her; she ran to me. 'Tazia knew she was safe in the hands of her Hanma.

When we recognize the enemy for who he is, we can call on the name of Jesus Christ to protect us. Listen, we can hold onto the hands of "Our wonderful Father which art in Heaven, Hallowed be His name!"

We must hold onto God's hand *before* a storm comes into our lives. It's hard to reach for help once the storm has begun to rage in our life! What storms are you facing while you're reading this message? Be honest–do you feel like going on? Please don't give up! My mentor/friend Elder Burton D. Clemons told us not to forget about our past victories! God will do what He says He will do. As we learn how to trust Him, we can relax and rest in Him. When my strength failed, He carried me through the storms of my life. When I tried to carry Miss 'Tazia my strength failed. I know God's strength will never fail. He will carry us until we're strong enough to walk on our own, but He won't leave us alone!

Chapter 3

It's all Good!

God, You Said!

While listening to Pastor Joel Osteen, my creative juices began to flow. He talked about the vacation he and his family took to Disney World. When they returned home, his daughter Alexandria asked him if they could go back to Disney World, and he told her yes. After some time had passed, she began to ask him about the promise he made to her. She didn't give up on her dream. She knew her daddy would keep his promise. Pastor Joel laughed and said he and his family would be going to Disney World after the morning service.

Pastor Joel talked about his sister and her husband's desire to have a child. She drew up a contract which she and her husband signed, and then they presented it to the Lord. He rewarded their act of faith by blessing them with twins. That's not the end of an extraordinary testimony. God blessed them with another miracle baby. They were blessed beyond their expectations.

He moved on to the story of the widowed woman in Luke 18:1-6. She went before a judge who didn't fear God or man. She expected the judge to avenge her of her adversaries. He didn't care about the woman or her issues. She wasn't about to be ignored and was determined to get what she asked for. The judge was tired of the woman getting on his nerves, so he told them to give her what she wanted.

Pastor Joel said, "We will get God's attention when we repeat His word back to Him! He must honor His word! We won't conquer our trials if we sit around and complain about them." I'm about to start my own "God, you said" list!

When I'm facing the storms of my life, God, you said you would never leave me or forsake me (Hebrews 13:5). When it seems as if my needs won't be met, I will declare Philippians 4:19, back to you. "But my God shall supply all of your needs according to His riches in glory by Christ Jesus." When my body is being attacked by illnesses, God, you said, "Many are the afflictions of the righteous, but the Lord delivers him out of them all" (Psalms 34:19).

When I'm trying to understand things which don't make sense, God, you said, "Trust in the Lord with all your heart, and lean not to thy own understanding" (Proverbs 3:5). God, you said, "When the enemy comes in like a flood, The Spirit of the Lord will lift up a standard against him" (Isaiah 59:19).

When other women are looking for a husband, I will stay in my place and wait. God, you said, "He who finds a wife finds a good thing, and obtains favor from the Lord" (Proverbs 18:22). When spirits of fear come against me, God, you said, "For God has not given us a spirit of fear, but of power, love, and of a sound mind" (II Timothy 1:7).

When we delight ourselves in God, He will give us the desires of our heart. We must not forget we are children of the Most High. We can remind God of what He said. He will be there for us when no one else is there for us. He's not destitute. He's not between a rock and a hard place. When we bless God by quoting His word back to Him, He will bless us beyond anything we can imagine!

Dry Bones, Get Up and Live!

After I had prayed and eaten my breakfast, my thoughts took me to the valley of dry bones found in Ezekiel 37:1-14. Get ready to enjoy the word of God with me. "The hand of the Lord was upon me and brought me out in the spirit of the Lord, and set me down in the midst of the valley; and it was full of bones." When Ezekiel looked around the valley, the dry bones were scattered all around him. He told God the bones were very dry. It was meant for him to see them in their pre-miracle state.

God asked Ezekiel a question (vs. 3). "And He said to me, 'Son of man, can these bones live?'" Ezekiel said, "O Lord God, thou knowest." God was about to show Ezekiel the power of His word. When God spoke to him again it was in the form of a command, not a question (vs. 4). "Again He said to me, 'Prophesy to these bones and say to them, O dry bones hear the word of the Lord!'" When Ezekiel prophesied to the dry bones, something strange began to happen.

A loud noise began to circulate throughout the valley of dry bones. As the dry bones began to come together, the muscles and skin began to wrap around the dry bones. God was about to breathe life into what was dead. We read in vs. 9 that He also said to Ezekiel, "Prophesy to the breath, prophesy, son of man, and say to the breath, 'Thus says the Lord God: Come from the four winds, O breath, and breathe on these slain, that they may live.'" The breath of life rose up in the mighty warriors who had fallen in battle. Now, they were about to stand up together again as a mighty army of God. Just as I was feasting on what God was giving me, He took me to vs. 11: Then He said to Ezekiel "Son of man, these bones are the whole house of Israel. They indeed say, 'Our bones are dry, and our hope is lost, and we ourselves are cut off.'" The feast of God isn't over, read vs. 12: "Therefore prophesy and say to them, 'Thus says the Lord God: Behold, O my people, I will open up your graves and cause you to come up from your graves, and bring you into the land of Israel.'"

God told Ezekiel to tell His people He was the one who took them out of their graves. He's the one who breathed life into their lifeless bodies. He wanted His people to get up and live! He's telling us to get up and live an abundant life. We can enjoy the promises which He's made us in due season. God will take us out of our graves of worry and doubt. We must speak life into what should live. We must speak death to the things that must die, forever!

If you smelled a foul odor in your house, wouldn't you look for the source of the odor? If the foul odor is found in the refrigerator, it must be cleaned out after the spoiled food is removed.

In a different example, if a dead animal is the source of a foul smell, it must be removed and the area must be sanitized. Death has a distinctive stench! Dead things must be disposed of one way or another. When God takes us out of our grave, He will take away the stench of death! He took Ezekiel on an unimaginable adventure. He was not the same after such a miraculous experience. One precious moment with God can change our lives forever. When God speaks life into us, we can live. Amen!

Convicted, Convinced, and Converted!

The words convicted, convinced, and converted should challenge us to get real! If any part of this message doesn't apply to you, just eat the meat and spit out the bones. I truly need every word of this message. It has allowed me to see my faults and the things I must change. If we see ourselves and don't change, we may miss the mark.

Some people are cold and deadly; it seems as if they were born without a conscience. Our world has become infested with sin. The value of life has diminished like the dollar bill! Can anyone still hear the voice of conviction? I clearly heard it when I was about twenty-four years old. My form of godliness was about to set me up to be delivered. When my mother-in-law Eleanor forgot to pick me up for church, I walked down to the neighborhood church. The ushers greeted me at the door with their smiles and their words of kindness. I didn't know when I walked into the doors of "The Tower of Prayer COGIC" it would become my church home for over twenty years.

When I sat down and looked around at the people who were rejoicing, I laughed. This wasn't the form of godliness I was used to. The praise and worship I used to offer up to God was as phony as a "pleather" coat or shoes that will crack in any weather. Wait until you read about my pathetic need to be seen and heard. I took the invitation to speak as a visitor too far! I asked if I could come to the front of the church to sing a solo. Yes, I really did ask for an open door to show off.

God used the words of the song by Danibelle to set me up to be delivered! "Many years ago, I was shown the way to go, but I just laughed and walked away. But as the time went by, I discovered I was wrong, I could not face another day. So then I humbled myself and prayed to God above, I'll remember the day, when Jesus Christ, washed my sins away." What a wonderful set up. I still laugh when I reflect back to that infamous moment. The spirit of conviction showed me I needed to be saved. I walked into the church for a quick emotional fix, not to be saved. When Pastor Clemons said, "If anyone needs prayer, they can come to the altar," it caught me off guard. I began to weep uncontrollably as I made my way down to the altar. It was time to repent, not show off. God saved me and filled me with His precious Holy Ghost. My life was about to be changed in a way that still amazes me.

When I was baptized in the past, I went down into the water as a dry sinner and came up and out of the water as a wet sinner. Listen: if we cover up our sins, we won't prosper. I have a praise report! My conviction convinced me it was time to be converted into a real Christian. God instructed Elder Clemons to take me in under watch care. Was it because of my past church-hopping? If I told you I never left my church, that statement would be a lie. When I came back, I had to conquer what I didn't deal with before I went missing in action.

God began to teach me how to love people who were difficult to like. He taught me how to hold on to

Him during the most difficult times of my life. He said, "Growing pains at any age are so painful." What a sweet revelation! I'm grateful for the love and support which my children and I received from our church family. We laughed, cried, and prayed together as a family. Being convicted, convinced, and converted has been an interesting journey. My journey isn't over, but I declare the worst is over and the best is yet to come!

The Lord spoke to me about premeditated sins! He was talking about preplanned sin! After the sin is committed, the sinner has planned to ask God to forgive them later. What if later comes sooner than you expected, and you don't get another chance to repent? Is your premeditated sin worth eternal damnation?

My difficult seasons have taught me how to be real. I won't paint you a portrait of a lady who has it all together. The choices I made as a sinner left scars on my life. I truly hope and pray someone will learn from my mistakes. I choose to give God my best today, just in case I don't see another tomorrow. I declare it shall be well with my soul.

As a new saint of God, I was encouraged by the lyrics of a simple song: "You will never be the same again; you will never be the same again, when Jesus steps in, new life will begin, you will never be the same again." A new life won't begin if we don't totally allow Jesus to come into our life. The devil will tell us we don't need to change the way we're living. If we entertain the lies of the liar, we'll end up in hell with him. I enjoyed my life as a sinner until Jesus saved me. Now, I'm enjoying my guilt-free life as a real Christian. If you still haven't been convicted, convinced, and converted to live for God, I hope someone is still praying for you! Somebody prayed for me!

Absent or Present!

It's about 4:30 in the morning and I can't go back to sleep. I can feel the presence of God; He wants to tell me something. As I was basking in His presence, I reflected back to my former school days. Each teacher was given a roster; it contained the names of the students that were assigned to their classroom. When the teacher called our name, we had to raise our hand and say, "present." If we weren't in the classroom when our name was called, we would be marked absent. If we came in after the roster was turned in to the office, the absent mark may or may not be corrected.

When we leave this world to face our judgment, the verdict will be final. There won't be any corrections. Hebrews 9:27 reads, "And as it is appointed unto men to die, but after this the judgment." We will spend eternity somewhere. If we live right, we'll be alright according to II Corinthians

5:8, which says, "We are confident, yes, well pleased rather to be absent from the body and to be present with the Lord." This is the only time when being absent won't be counted against us.

My school day reflection won't take long, for another message is on the way. One of the young ladies in our band class was late most of the time. She came up with the most comical reasons for being late. Our band teacher voiced his amusement or lack of amusement as she made excuses for being late. As we grow up, we must put our childish behavior behind us. If we don't change our behavior, we'll be judged by our past behavior. My school day reflections are over. It's time to address some church issues. Some of my thoughts may be comical, or some may shock you. It may affirm where you stand with God!

The first issue on my list is the church roll, which constantly changed for various reasons. Before I move on, there's something I need to confess. My name was on too many church rolls; I church-hopped a lot. This is what happened. When the preacher delivered a message that convicted me, it messed me up. When the doors of the church were opened up, it appealed to my emotions. The tears that ran down my face were real. I really did want to do the right thing at that emotional moment. I liked hearing, "The right hand of fellowship has been extended to Sis Pam." I was now a true member of___, whatever church I had hopped to! I liked being called Sis Pam, even if I didn't live up to the respectable title.

Let me tell you about the so-called sister I ticked off during choir rehearsal. When she started running her foul, trash-talking mouth, I tried to ignore her. Miss Big Mouth was talking her way into a beat down, one threat at a time. After choir rehearsal was over, she snatched a handful of my long beautiful glory. She held on to it as if it was a lifeline. The shocked choir members that stepped in between us made her let go of my hair. I wasn't saved at the time, but I refused to fight the glory-snatcher in church. She refused to meet me out in the church parking lot.

I wanted to bust her in the mouth, to shut her up, and get her good for snatching my hair. When we cooled off, she apologized for her trash-talking, glory-snatching drama. I apologized for my "Come outside to the church parking lot, I've got something for you" drama. If we had fought in the church or the parking lot, God would not have been pleased. The devil would have been glorified. Things went okay for a while, until I realized that something was wrong. Most of us, including the preacher, weren't living a life that pleased God. I must deliver this message, one truth at a time. Just as I was about to church hop for the last time, God showed me something.

My problem wasn't with the preacher, the glory-snatcher, or the rest of the congregation. The woman in the mirror was my biggest problem. I needed to truly repent and get right with God. My church-hopping stopped when I attended a church service at the Tower of Prayer COGIC. *My* form of godliness hadn't been satisfying my hunger for God; I needed to know Him for real.

I'm about to throw out some lifelines. Catch them and hold on to them until your help arrives! If our names aren't written in the Lamb's book of life, a listing of our names on a church roll won't matter! We are told in the Word of God to occupy until Jesus returns. Well, guess what–occupying a church pew won't secure you a place in heaven when Jesus returns. I'm trying to remember the lyrics of an old school song; okay, here it is: "It's yo thang, do whatcha wanna do, I can't tell ya who to sock it to." The grammar is incorrect, but the message is clear. "If you continue to sin, do what you do well, your wages of your sin, will send you straight to hell."

This isn't a message of gloom and doom. We must wake up and keep it real. When we see ourselves, are we willing to change what must be changed? My mentor/friend, Mother Gene Woo-Clemons, is known for her declaration, "Devil, I see you." We must use the word of God to destroy the works of the enemy. When this life is over and we're absent from our body, we can be present with the Lord.

One Day at a Time

As I was relaxing on my front porch, it occurred to me that many of my various inspirational messages have been written here. Our lives are forever changing right in front of our eyes. Will the goals we set be met, or will they be put on the bottom of our "to-do list?" As long as we live, we should want to grow. If we put God first in our lives, everything will be worked out together for our good. This message is a rewrite from May 22nd, 2002. God is taking me into a new direction, so here's the rewrite:

If you weren't born with a silver spoon in your mouth, you climbed up your ladder of success one rung at a time. How many people are willing to climb over other people to reach their level of success? As I previously quoted in another chapter, my grandmother said, "Every bird that flies high has to come down for a drink of water."

What do we see when we evaluate our lives? In the words of my friend Shelly Moorer, "If the truth be told, most of us need to grow up." I don't mind talking about my faults. I hope what I'm about to reveal will help somebody. I took too many precious relationships for granted. Some of the damage I caused can't be fixed. Death came in and took some of my loved ones. I'm working on relationships that <u>can</u> be fixed. I've tried to apologize to a few people, but they refused to accept my apology. They made sure I knew the words "I'm sorry" couldn't fix the pain I caused. I owned up to the pain I caused, but it didn't matter to the people who refuse to forgive me. I'm not trying to be insensitive or mean, but if they're not willing to forgive me, *they* won't be forgiven!

My friend/mentor, Marion Gene Woo-Clemons, testified about an apology that wasn't accepted well. I need to call her to make sure my facts are correct. Okay, I'm back. This is what she told me: While she and her grandchildren were out running errands, she bought them an ice-cream cone. As she reached over to get something, she knocked Brandon's ice-cream cone on the floor of the car. At the time of the ice-cream mishap, he was about four or five years old. He looked down at his ruined treat as Mother Clemons tried to apologize to him. With tears running down his face, Brandon said, "Some things sorry helps and some things it don't." Do we hear what our children are or aren't saying? I will store Brandon's raw quote with the rich nuggets I've collected over the years. A replacement cone could melt his disappointment one lick at a time. Some issues can't be fixed, like the ice-cream cone mishap. I found a flyer on the floor of my apartment building that said, "Yesterday is History, Tomorrow is a Mystery, so live today!" It was meant for me to find the flyer. I encourage you to enjoy today, for tomorrow may not come.

When I attended the Tower of Prayer COGIC, I met one of the most powerful seasoned saints. Mother Sarah A. Thompson was loved and highly respected. I didn't always agree with what she said, but I respected her right to say what she needed to say! She loved the word of God and His people. St. Matthew 6:33 was one of her favorite scriptures. "But seek ye first the kingdom of God and His righteousness, and all these things will be added unto you." Mother Thompson taught us how to put God first. I enjoyed hearing her sing, "One Day at a Time." Her anointed voice blessed so many people. She truly lived a holy life both inside and outside of the church walls.

If we seek God one day at a time, He'll take care of our needs and us. He created the creatures and living things on the earth, one day at a time! As we're weaving our way through life, do we really appreciate how blessed we are? We can't afford to take life or relationships for granted. If we learn from our mistakes, it's a gain, not a loss. When we hear the words, "Well done, thou good and faithful servant; enter into the joy of the Lord," everything that was wrong will be made right!

I Will Laugh Again!

This message completely took me by surprise! While I was talking to someone, I heard "I will laugh again." When we face hard trials, it can create a battlefield in our mind! We may feel as if our broken heart may stop beating any second. When we face a medical issue, we may be asked to rate our pain on a scale of one to ten. This question is asked so our medical issue can be assessed. Can any of our emotional pain be measured on a scale of one to ten? No it can't!

Just as the message was starting to flow, I decided to take a break. As I was about to get back to work, my phone rang. My Aunt, Barbara Hale, was calling to tell me her niece died. We had recently buried my brother Calvin. Our sister Wyonna (Marie) fought a battle she could no longer fight. As I was listening to my Aunt Barbara, God gave me what to tell her. I told her the

Holy Ghost would truly comfort her during her process of grieving and healing. Tears and laughter are a vital part of her healing process. Yes, Auntie, in time you will laugh again. When we face difficult trials, will we bless the Lord at all times? Or will we blame Him for what we're going through?

Have you ever felt as if you would never laugh again? I did, but we know the devil is a liar! The medicine of laughter is from God, so you can't overdose on it. Let me ask you something. Do you remember the last time you took a good laugh break? We're about to take one right now. Think back on something or someone who made you laugh. Close your eyes, and focus on that funny moment. Enjoy that wonderful moment as long as you can. I just did what I told you to do. I took a large dose of medicine, and it was so good. I couldn't stay in the moment, for who would finish the message? We must take as many laugh breaks as possible. Have any of you ever laughed and cried at the same time? Is it possible to feel joy and pain at the same time? I'm about to answer those questions!

A few years ago, I attended the home going service for First Lady Dr. Sherilyn Smith's mother. Mother Joanne was truly loved. The look of sadness in her loved ones' eyes said what they couldn't say. Her family knew their loss was a gain for the kingdom of heaven. I saw the tears that flowed as loved ones tried to cope with their pain. When humorous memories of Mother Joanne were shared, laughter broke out throughout the sanctuary. I was truly humbled as I listened to the reflections of such an extraordinary lady. I'm sorry I never got a chance to know her, but I can lock the testimonies about her in my heart.

Dear First Lady Sherilyn, this special moment is for you, and it's from the heart of God! You will reap the goodness that you have sown. You have faithfully ministered in so many lives such as my family and me. You will be honored and respected for who you are. God has crowned your head with an abundance of wisdom. You have found favor with Him. He has armed you with the truth. Keep on speaking the truth, even when it's not received. Shake the dust off and keep moving in the strength of the Lord. You are God's chosen vessel for such a time as this. It may appear as if the weariness of life will shut you down and shut you up. Not so! God's joy will strengthen you when you need it the most.

When First Lady Serita Jakes lost her mother, she shared the things Bishop Jakes did for her during her grieving process. She said when he proclaimed the word of God, it ushered her into the presence of the Lord. I hear you, Holy Ghost! When Bishop Smith began to eulogize his first and only First Lady Sherilyn's mother, he tenderly ushered her into the presence of the Lord. May God wrap His loving arms around you as you hurt and heal!

God will turn our sadness into gladness. He can collect tears that we can't contain. He will turn our precious moments into precious memories. He'll give us joy when we're not happy about what we're going through. Light chases away darkness. Laughter can chase away sadness. If we incorporate the light of Jesus, the joy of the Lord, with the medicine of laughter, we can make it through anything.

Are you ready to take another laugh break with me? I'm about to share an embarrassing moment with you. As I was standing in the side aisle of the sanctuary, a minister started laughing when he walked past me. He wouldn't look at me, though; he looked straight ahead as he went to the restroom. It came to me to look down. I froze when I looked down and saw my skirt on the floor. My bountiful body was partially covered up. In my haste to get ready for church, I had forgotten to fasten my skirt. I just stood in the isle trying to regroup from the shock.

What was I going to do? I didn't want anyone else to see my exposed body. Mother Derrington-Butler had just told us we should always wear a slip under our garments. In my mind, there was no reason to wear a slip under a lined garment. The fresh, wise words of Mother D. instantly came back to me. I'm so glad I wore the suit that had a long jacket–it covered most of my body. I couldn't bend over to pick my skirt off the floor, so I quickly scooted over and sat down in the closest pew. Keep in mind my skirt was still on the floor. I finally got Missionary Renee Thompson's attention. When my dear friend/sister came over and saw my skirt on the floor, she laughed as she handed me my skirt. Renee and some of my other sisters/friends shielded me as I put my skirt back on. I regained my skirt, but my dignity was still on the floor. I made sure there wouldn't be another wardrobe malfunction.

When Mother Derrington found out about my skirt drama, she just shook her head and laughed. I wanted to ask my amused brother why he didn't say, "Hey sister Pam, you might want to get your skirt off the floor." He just walked by and left it on the floor- how rude! I'm able to laugh at my embarrassing moments. If I could show you a video of my life, it would make a standup comedian sit back down!

Some people think it's wrong to laugh while you're grieving. I can't think of a better time to enjoy the medicine of laughter. Just as I was finishing up this message, I received a 911 phone call from my daughter Brandy. Her phone call shook me up for a moment. I dealt with my emotions, and then I reflected back on the goodness of God. I told her God would see her and her children through the storm that had come into their lives. She isn't able to laugh right now, but in time she will laugh again!

The joy of the Lord will strengthen us when happiness slips away. I closed my eyes and thought about something my four-year-old grandchild Shailah said on our way home from church. As her mother Heather and I were talking, she blurted out, "Grandma gets the check, Grandma gets the car." I turned around and asked her what she said. When she repeated it, Heather and I laughed so hard. When I turned back to face my grandchild, I said, "I receive that!" Shailah didn't know about the checks I'm waiting for. I can't say too much around her, for she talks a lot. She does know that I want a Kia Soul. Whenever she sees one she points it out and says, "There's Grandma's car."

Amen, baby! We were still laughing when my daughter said, "What about Mommy?" Shailah answered, "Umm," as if to say I've got nothing for you right now. We burst out laughing again. There are so many more "wow" moments, but you get the message. God wants us to know He's there for us when we laugh *and* when we cry! Close your eyes for a moment. Let the joy of laughter wrap around you like a soft warm hug from God. I'm about to close, so take your time and enjoy your precious moments.

Chapter 4

The Devil is a Lie, and a Liar!

I Get Down for Mine!

Does the phrase "I get down for mine" suggest that some people are willing to fight for their loved ones? Yes it does. Just give me a few moments of your time so I can tell you what inspired me to write this message. The people I'm going to tell you about are living on the edge of danger.

My daughter Brandy and I were enjoying some mother-daughter moments on her deck. All of a sudden, her neighbor and family ran out of the front door. They jumped into their cars and sped off down the street. When they came back, they got out of their car, laughing and talking about their adventure. The woman came over to tell us that someone had stolen a bike off her front porch. They chased the bicycle thief down and recovered the stolen bike.

When I gave her my signature are-you-serious look, the woman laughed and said, "I get down for mine." She and her foolish posse went looking for trouble. It's easy to get into trouble, but it's hard to get out of trouble. What if the bicycle thief pulled out a gun while they were chasing him? What if he had a posse of his own? A bike can be replaced, but a life can't be replaced. Brandy and I shook our heads in disbelief as the "I get down for mine" posse' continued to celebrate their victory. I hope and pray that they don't end up in jail or at a morgue with a tag on their toe!

I'm taking the "I get down for mine" declaration to another level. We get down for our loved ones when we pray for them! If we release our loved ones to God, He'll take good care of them! We must pray for those who hurt them. The bible clearly tells us vengeance belongs to the Lord. He will vindicate us if we stay out of His way. If we retaliate against those who have wronged us, God will deal with us!

As a child, I was forced to fight people who didn't like me. I tried to avoid confrontations. I was a dreamer and a class clown; I wasn't a fighter. I didn't have an "I get down for mine" posse." I had to give my opponent a beat down, or take a beat down. If my opponent took a beat down, the fickle crowd cheered for me. If I took a beat down, they teased me.

When we get down and pray for our loved ones, God will work it out for them. He will right the wrong. If we go down fighting a battle for our loved ones without Him, we may not get back up! I choose to get down for mine by leaving them in the capable hands of the Lord!

I Don't Receive That!

Let me get straight to the point-why do we accept what we should reject? Does it have anything to do with how we feel about ourselves? When I look back over my life, I can't believe what I used to put up with. I just wanted to be loved and accepted. I didn't love myself or see my worth, so I took what I thought I deserved! Wow, as I was typing that last sentence, it really got to me. When we get a revelation from God, how will we handle it? I'm about to let it soak in as I'm finishing up this message.

Ladies, I need to talk with you for a moment. Men, don't feel left out; you're important too! In one of his messages, Bishop T. D. Jakes said women are receivers. He said, "Women should watch what they're receiving." If we allow God to guard our heart, mind, and our finances, we'll repel what we used to accept. Ladies, watch out for the tall, short, dark, or light counterfeit men. They're phonier than a three-dollar bill.

Wow, God just showed me something else. If we put clean and dirty water together on a surface, a sponge or a mop can't separate the clean water from the dirty water. Ladies, do you hear what He's telling us? He loves us dearly and He wants what's best for us. If a tall or short man is no good, he's just no good. Please leave him standing alone in the need of much prayer. Men, this is for you: if a tall, short, dark or light, pretentious woman isn't God's choice for you, leave her in the hands of the Lord!

When God began to show me how some of my friends felt about me, it messed me up. I had to accept what had been revealed to me. If we intend to receive what He has for us, there must be a renewing of our mind. Romans 12:2 reads, "And do not be conformed to this world, but be transformed by the renewing of your mind that you may prove what is that good and acceptable and perfect will of God."

My dearest friend and missionary, Angela P. Wilson, is as real as it gets. She'll tell you what you may or may not want to hear. Let me give you an example of her uniqueness. In one of our conversations, I was venting about a few opinionated people. All of a sudden, Angie blurted out, "Aw, girl, just eat the meat and spit out the bones." When she repeated that, we laughed. Did you know laugher has the power to defuse anger? It can also chase away sadness. When we overcome our adversities, they won't overcome us. We must be open to receive what God has for us.

When someone tried to speak something negative into Angie's life, she said, "I don't receive that!" It took courage for her to rebuke what was said to her. I love Angie and her rawness! She deals with life in such a unique way. I surround myself with people like her. I'm talking about people who will speak the truth, even if it's not received. It's time for me to do some drastic house cleaning. One-sided friendships are unacceptable. In the words of Popeye, "I stood all I cans stans and I can't stans no more." God's showing me people as they are, not as I choose to see them.

When someone tries to speak something negative into my life, I smile and say, "I don't receive that." The smile on my face doesn't mean I don't mean what I said. Whatever is in a person will come out sooner or later! My Grandma Estella often said, "What don't come out in the wash will come out in the rinse." I'm working on me. I don't have time to work on how someone feels about me. I still get frustrated by the actions of others. I'm growing up one issue at a time. You will be able to read about my ups and my downs as I walk with the Lord.

I have some of the most unusual, anointed, and gifted brothers and sisters in the Lord. Trust me; they keep me grounded. Let me tell you about India Wade. She's armed and dangerous. The true anointing on her life gives her the authority to boldly go where unarmed people better not go. When she gives out what God has given her, she moves on to the next assignment. You can accept what she has given you or you can reject it;

that's between you and God! I finally crossed the line one day and got on her nerves. Just as I was about to vent about one of God's children, I heard India say, "Listen, Pam." I knew I was about to get checked. She said, "You are letting your past hold you back. You need to let it go!" God used her to tell me the truth. If you're not ready to hear the truth, don't mess with India. The Holy Ghost in her will show you how to get it together!

Did you ever think the world would be a better place if God wiped some people off the face of the earth? He may not change the people who are difficult for you to like, but *He's able to change the way you feel about them.* If any of my previous statements don't sound spiritual, don't forget that God is still working on me. We have the right to reject what He doesn't want us to receive! When a few people said they were going to curse my life, the Holy Ghost shut that lie down. He said no one could curse my life because He has blessed my life. When you mess with me, my daddy will get you!

When the enemy is allowed to plant seeds of deception in our minds, they will grow like unattended weeds. We blame many of our poor choices on the enemy. God will hold us accountable for the choices that we have made. Do any of you remember a ride called the seesaw? My friends and I played on the carefree ride. It took us up and down until we got bored. We can't afford to ride on the seesaw of wise or foolish decisions. If we allow God to lead us in the right direction, we will make the right choices.

When we mess up, yes, I said when we mess up, we'd better repent and get it right before it's too late. If we continue to accept what we should reject, we will miss out on what God truly has in store for us. When He told me that my blessed life couldn't be cursed, it encouraged me! He assured me that I am His and He has me covered. Don't let anyone speak anything into your life that doesn't come from God!

Shut the Pity Party Down!

As the old year was about to end, I cleaned my apartment and did my laundry. My lack of planning left me home alone, not at church. I have no problem confessing the truth. While I was doing a soul search, a sneaky, filthy spirit of depression slammed me real hard. I'm giving it to you as it happened! When the ball dropped on Times Square in New York, so did my mood. People began to kiss and embrace one another. Really, how could they celebrate while I was home alone?

My pity party got more pitiful when I thought about the times I spent alone. Who gets married to be left home alone? I guess I did, but I refused to cry about the loneliness I had not given to God. No one came to my pathetic pity party. My friends or family members were at church or out doing what they do.

Okay, I'm shutting this raggedy, pitiful pity party down. Why wasn't the end of a challenging year enough of a reason to celebrate? How dare I start off a New Year with an old mess? It's time to change my attitude. I'm ready to trust God to do what's best for me, with or without a husband!

I'm giving myself permission to celebrate who I am in God. I'm about to enjoy my life as a unique single woman. Married people wonder why they got married, as single people are wondering why we aren't married. I will wait for God to send His choice for me into my life. I'm not about to write, "The honeymoon is over, the divorce is final" part two, three, or four, and so on!

God won't leave me alone, even when loneliness comes for a visit. No one will ever love me like Him. He's wonderful, gentle, kind, compassionate, and wise. He guards my heart and my mind. He's the reason why "all is well with my soul." Hey Daddy, wasn't that good? I hope it went straight to your heart! It's from your child Pam. Am I not the apple of your eye? Yes I am! I called on Jesus Christ to shut the pathetic pity party down. Unresolved issues will set us up to accept the spirit of pity, misery, fear, and depression.

When we face the truth, will we change what must be changed? Will we accept what we can't change? I got my breakthrough! Are you still with me? Are you ready to be set free? Just as we cheer for other people, we must cheer for ourselves. I will celebrate God and the wonderful life He has for me! Let me get the celebration started. When I think of the goodness of Jesus and all that He's done for me, my soul cries out Halleluiah! I thank God for saving me! It's time to go, it's time to celebrate!

Get Ready, a Storm is Coming!

Whenever the news is reported, it includes a weather report given by a trained meteorologist. The weather report may include a forecast of sunshine, rain, snow, or even a storm warning. Whenever a storm warning is issued for a designated area, some people choose to ignore the warning. Why are they willing to risk their life and the lives of others by trying to protect their possessions? I don't know; they seem to value their possessions more than their life! Wouldn't it be terrible if their things survived, but they perished in the storm? That's something to think about.

In the days of Noah, God told him He was about to destroy the earth with a flood (Genesis 6:17). "And behold, I, even I, do bring a flood of water upon the earth, to destroy all flesh, wherein, is the breath of life, from under the heaven: and everything that is in the earth shall die." Noah found favor with God, so He spared him, his family, and two of every living creature. I can't understand why the creepy, cold-blooded snakes were included in the two by two! Noah was instructed to build an ark according to the directions God gave him. Noah obeyed Him, even when it didn't seem to make sense.

Try to imagine how the people reacted when Noah began to build the ark. When he said, "It's going to rain," they thought he was crazy because it had never rained! Now stay with me while a picture is being painted, one brush stroke at a time. The ark has been completed; Noah, his family, and the animals were loaded onto the ark. The people were still laughing and mocking him. God shut the door of the ark. The laughter stopped when it began to rain. Death snatched the mockers like a thief in the night. There was nowhere for the doomed people to hide. The entire earth was covered with water.

When the flood was over, God dried off the earth for Noah, his family, and the animals in the ark. After the flood was over, God said that He would not send another flood to destroy the earth. God placed a beautiful rainbow in the sky to seal the promise He made to Noah and the future generations.

As I was on my way to a job that I no longer enjoyed, God did something wonderful for me. The horrific pain that I was going through seemed as if it would never end! My life was in turmoil. I couldn't find any peace at home, church, or at work. I cried all the way to work! When I stopped at a stop sign, I heard the words, "Look up." When I looked up at the sky, I saw the most beautiful, vibrant rainbow.

God said, "I will never allow a storm to destroy you!" He didn't say the storms wouldn't come into my life. He promised to keep me safe during my storms. I believe He placed the beautiful rainbow in the sky just for me. He showed me I could always depend on Him in spite of what happened in my life. While I was finishing up this message, I took a break. When I stepped out on my balcony and looked up at the sky, I saw another beautiful rainbow from my Promise

Keeper. After the sighting of the rainbow, I was inspired to keep on writing!

God will keep His promises as He keeps us safe when the enemy comes against us (Isaiah 59:19). "So that they may fear the name of the Lord from the east and the west, and His glory from the rising of the sun; when the enemy shall come in like a flood, the Spirit of the Lord will lift up a standard against him." When God's standard is lifted up against the enemy, he must flee from us for a season.

The storms of life show us what we're made of! We must learn how to trust God before a storm comes into our life. He will keep us calm during the storm that is raging in our life! Whenever a natural storm is over, how do the survivors make sense of the devastation? As they sadly sift through the rubble, the dazed look on their faces shows what they're not able to say! Will the area destroyed by a storm be declared a disaster area? How will the survivors rebuild their lives that were ripped apart by the storm? The grieving process and the healing process can't be rushed. We all deal with devastations in our own way. The enemy of our soul is lurking around to see what the storm has done *to* us. When he sees what the storm has done *for* us, it will confuse him.

Before I close this message, I want to share a powerful testimony with you from Mother Leona Derrington-Butler. This incredible woman of God spent the majority of her life serving Him and His people. No matter what she was going through, she still encouraged anyone she came in contact with. Mother Butler told me about the really nice house she and her children moved into. She loved the house, but she didn't like the kitchen. After she told God about the issue she had with kitchen, it caught on fire. Don't waste a sad moment on her or her children. She praised and worshipped God, in spite of what they were going through. He rewarded them with a brand new kitchen complete with new appliances. No test, no testimony. The storm that came into their lives didn't come to stay.

When a storm warning is issued, don't assume the storm will pass over and miss your area. Seek out a safe shelter until the storm is over. If you don't find a shelter from the storm, you may not live to ignore another warning! Take shelter from storms and live to tell someone how God took care of you in the midst of the storm!

Where Does It Hurt?

I was given this message a few years ago, but it was stored away along with other inspirational messages. The "where does it hurt" question reminded me of my countless trips to the emergency room. The triage nurses asked a series of questions as they were taking my vitals. If I was in pain, they asked me to rate my pain. "On a scale of one to ten, ten being the worst, how would you rate your pain?"

The location and level of the pain determined when a doctor would see me. I have lain in the emergency room for hours in tremendous pain. I've listened to frustrated patients or their loved ones as they also waited for a doctor to come into the room. When you're hurting, you just want the pain to stop. On one of my trips to the E.R, I witnessed an argument between a doctor and a patient. The patient went off about the medication that had been prescribed for his dental pain.

He told the doctor, "I wish you could feel my pain." She said, "You will not talk to me like that." She told him that his issue had to be addressed by a dentist. The doctor said, "If you don't settle down, you will be escorted out of the hospital. The irritated man refused to shut up and continued to go off until a policeman walked into the examining room. He listened to the man for a moment and then he said, "You're the one who came here to be helped." If we foolishly bite the hand that feeds us, who will feed us when we're hungry? Was the man in that much pain, or was he trying to get the good stuff?

On one of my most painful trips to the emergency room, my pain went beyond a ten! After the doctor examined me, he asked me if I wanted something for pain. I said, "No, I want you to find out what's wrong with me." I refused to be seen and treated as just another slick patient who came to the hospital to get pain medication.

When he was leaving my room, he turned around and said, "We're going to do our best to find out what's wrong with you." When my test results came back, they revealed the source of my problem. The pain was excruciating, but I didn't cry. All right, I've proven my point. Now, where's the doctor? I'm ready to take whatever pain medicine you want me have.

Our emotional pain can't be measured on a scale of one to ten. How do we deal with the pain we can't talk about? We give it to the one who can handle it. God can heal us when we're hurting. He has the ability to reach us where we are. He does care about what we're going through. Didn't He send His only Son, Jesus Christ, to prove His love for us? None of us could have endured what Jesus went through. He was rejected, betrayed, beaten, tortured, and humiliated. He endured indescribable pain as He took our sins to the cross.

While I was finishing up this message, I took a break. During the break, God led me to call several people to share a portion of this message with them. I told them to give their pain, disappointment, and their doubt to God. Are we willing to hear Him when we're hurting beyond our endurance? He's the only one who can heal us of the pain that will come into our lives.

What are you facing as you're reading this? Keep in mind there is nothing too hard for God. Remind Him of what He has spoken in his precious word. Give Him your pain. He can release you to live an abundant life! You can't enjoy your future until you're released from your painful past. Cast all of your cares on Him; He will take wonderful care of you and your concerns!

Chapter 5

I Hear You, Daddy!

Enter Into His Gate!

"Enter into his gates with thanksgiving, And into His courts with praise. Be thankful to Him and bless His name" (Psalms 100: 4). Verse 5 reads, "For the Lord is good; His mercy is everlasting, and His truth endures to all generations." When we obey the voice and the word of God, it touches His heart. He deserves our love, honor, and respect.

Before entering a courtroom, you must pass through a metal detector. You may even be subjected to a body search. These checks are done to ensure the safety of anyone inside the courtroom. When we are in court, we are expected to act properly. No one is allowed to disrespect anyone inside of the courtroom□ *especially* the presiding judge! Disrespectful people will be escorted out of the courtroom and may even end up in jail.

Let me go back to the portion of scripture that talks about the gate of the Lord. What an honor to be invited into such a holy place. We have a personal invitation to commune with God. Our praises and worship will take us into the courts of the Lord. I found a few scriptures that blessed me. Here's the key to living a victorious life: (1) (Psalms 34:1-3) "I will bless the Lord at all times; His praise shall continually be in my mouth." (2) "My soul shall make a boast in the Lord; the humble shall hear thereof and be glad." When we boast about the goodness of God, our focus won't be on the deeds of the devil. (3) "Oh, magnify the Lord with me, and let us exalt His name together." When we magnify God and lift up His precious, holy name, our issues will be minimized.

We can't enter into God's court if we don't enter into His gate with thanksgiving! When we enter into the presence of God, we may not be able to utter a word. We must savor every moment with Him as if it may be our last!

The Bible is full of both wise and foolish people. We can learn from their victories or their defeats. Hannah was an unusual woman. She was married to Elkanah. She knew how to "enter into the gate of the Lord" with thanksgiving. Her desire to have a child caused her a great deal of heartbreak. Elkanah had another wife whose name was Peninnah. As she bore him children, she constantly rubbed her motherhood in Hannah's face. A child would certainly fill the void in Hannah's life. Her husband couldn't fix what he didn't understand. 1 Samuel 1:8 reads, "Then Elkanah her husband said to her, 'Hannah why do you weep? Why do you not eat? And why is your heart grieved? Am I not better than ten sons?'"

When Hannah went to the House of God, she made a vow to Him. She told Him if He gave her a son, she would dedicate him to the Lord. When Eli the priest saw Hannah, he assumed that she was drunk. The vow she made to God came from her heart, not her lips. Hannah explained to Eli what she faced as a barren woman. He told her to go in peace. He prayed that God would give her what she asked for.

Her prayer was answered. She gave birth to a baby boy and named him Samuel. Hannah didn't forget about the vow she had made to the Lord. After Samuel was weaned, she took him and an offering back to the House of the Lord. When they arrived at the temple, she reminded Eli of the vow she had made to God. Eli dedicated Samuel back to God. He was loaned to Hannah for a short time, but truly belonged to the Lord.

When we enter into the gate of the Lord with thanksgiving, seasons of lack will disappear. We will rebuke what we used to receive. When we enter, our inner beauty will radiate on our face. When we're asked about our outward glow, we'll be able to boast about the goodness of God. I praise Him for what He has allowed me to share with you. Get ready for the closing!

There were ten lepers who were declared unclean. If anyone came in contact with a leprous person, he or she could become contaminated. When Jesus healed the ten lepers, He told them to go to the priest. The priest had the authority to declare them clean. One of the former lepers turned around and thanked Jesus for his healing. He received a bonus for his gratitude! The former leper was made whole. The nine former lepers were healed, but they weren't made whole. I recently saw a credit card commercial that simply said, "What's in your wallet?" God isn't concerned about what's in our wallet. He's concerned about what's in our heart!

Stop, Look, and Listen!

While I was dealing with a business matter, I heard the phrase, "Stop, look and listen." God is changing the way that I write, so I'm often amazed when He uses me in such an unusual way. He now gives me what He wants me to know while I'm typing. I never liked to type until now. I've always regretted the time I wasted in my typing class. While my classmates were learning how to type, I chose to work on my skills as the class clown. My teacher didn't appreciate me using her classroom for my comedy routine. The students who laughed at my routine still managed to do their work. I flunked my typing class with a F5. My guardians assured me that they weren't amused with my bad grade or my bad behavior.

God's merciful to us even when we mess up! I'm about to tell you why I acted up in my typing class. I had a hard time learning the keyboard. I didn't ask my teacher to help me. I'm paying it forward by telling you, don't waste any teachable moments! You may not get another chance to get it right. When I look back over my past, my future is looking a whole lot better.

In school, we were taught how to stay safe, especially when it came to a train crossing. Before drivers crossed over a train track, they were supposed to stop, look, and listen for an approaching train. People who tried to beat a train usually lost the race! It's been said, "A picture is worth a thousand words." The mutilated vehicles we saw on the screen said enough!

The stop, look and listen lesson was branded in my mind. Just as we must obey the laws of the land, we'd better obey the word of God. When He speaks to us, do we really hear what He's saying?

I briefly thought back to the children of Israel. God protected them before and after He delivered them from the hands of their enemy. After they were set free, many of them focused on the life they left behind. When God parted the Red Sea, they didn't have time to "stop, look, or listen," for the enemy was pursuing them. After they crossed and stood on dry land, their enemies were swallowed up by the Red Sea as if they never existed. God can totally wipe out our enemies or He can set a table for us in the presence of our enemies. Our enemies won't be able to get up from the table while we're being blessed. My enemies will be sitting at my table until I'm called home or until Jesus comes back. The children of Israel were given another reason to rejoice. Their enemies could never hurt them again.

During the storms of life, we must <u>stop</u> and reflect on our past victories. We must <u>look</u> past the storms that are raging in our lives. We must <u>listen</u> to the voice of God and trust Him! Didn't He promise to keep us safe during our storms? Yes, He did. You can lock that promise in your heart. I was about to close the message until God gave me some more good stuff!

When Abraham's nephew, Lot, pitched his tent too close to the sin line, he and his family still found favor with God. The Lord warned Lot about His plan to destroy the entire city of Sodom and Gomorrah. The angels told Lot and his family to leave the city. They didn't move quickly enough, so the angels took them by their hands and led them out of the city. God is so merciful to us, even when we don't obey Him or His word, but let's not take His mercy or love for granted.

Lot and his family were told not to look back while Sodom and Gomorrah were being destroyed. His wife did stop to look back at the horrific destruction, and her foolish act of disobedience transformed her into a pillar of salt. Lot didn't turn back to face the same fate as his salty wife. He and the rest of his obedient family made it safely to their destination.

Are some of us like the foolish pillar of salt? Bad choices will mess us up sooner or later. Someone said, "If I was Lot's wife, I wouldn't have looked back." If you were his wife, you would have done just what she did!

The devil doesn't want us to heed what God is telling us. In the time it's taken me to type this line, he has set up traps to ensnare us. We must arm ourselves with the word of the Lord. When we focus on Him and

His word, we will "stop" focusing on the wrong things. When we "look" at God for whom He is, we won't glorify the enemy of our soul. When we "listen" to the voice of the Lord, we will tune out the voice of the enemy.

I hope you are inspired by this message. Are you honest enough to admit whether you do, or don't, have a relationship with God? If you don't have one, what are you waiting for? I'm taking a few moments to look over this message. I don't take any gift that has been loaned to me for granted. I'm making sure it's what God has given me to give to you. Yes, it is!

When God Calls Your Name!

I was working on the message "Where is it, Daddy?" until something caught my attention. When I glanced up at the television, a preview of the movie *The Easter Experience* was being televised. Mary, the woman whom Jesus set free, went to the tomb to look for His body. When she discovered His body was gone, it messed her up. When Jesus called her name, He got her attention. If God called our name at this very moment, what would we do?

Does anyone remember the commercial, "When E. F Hutton speaks, people listen?" When God speaks, we'd better listen to Him, especially when He calls our name. I could not get the words "when God calls your name" out of my mind. When Jesus called out to Peter, He asked Him if he loved Him – three times. When Peter answered Jesus for the last time, Jesus told him to feed His sheep.

After Jesus was told His friend Lazarus had died, He wept. He went to the place where he was entombed. Jesus called to Lazarus and told him to come forth. Out of the tomb came Lazarus, still wrapped in his death clothes, but very much alive! Can you imagine how he felt when he saw his loved ones rejoicing? When Jesus Christ called Lazarus out the tomb, He took away the stench of death!

God just said, "When I call your name, you can step out of your death clothes!" Jesus Christ stepped out of His death clothes over two thousand years ago. When God calls our name, there will be a change. When we answer His call and repent, we will become new, according to 1 Corinthians 5:17. "Therefore if any be in Christ, he is a new creature: old things are passed away; behold all things are become new."

My mother, Helen, named me Pamela Jean Coston. I choose to be called Pam, not Pamela. My mentor/friend Elder Burton D. Clemons and Minister Jonathon Wade call me Pammie. Not everyone has earned the right to call me Pammie. God can call me whatever He chooses to call me. When I was in the world, I was called names not listed on my birth certificate. In one of Mr. Tyler Perry's movies, the infamous Madea used an unforgettable quote. A young lady in the movie said the children at school called her names. Madea told the young lady, "You're not what people call you; you're who you answer to!" Amen! We must keep our ears open to the voice of God! When He calls our name, we must be ready to answer His call.

Their Strength is in Their Struggle!

When God told me to release my children to Him, I asked Him to clarify what he meant. I'll do my best to give you some good stuff to read. When a caterpillar is born, it isn't the prettiest or the strongest creature. As it begins to build a chrysalis (cocoon) around itself, the cocoon becomes its wall of protection. A wonderful transformation will take place inside of the chrysalis. When the time is right, out comes one of God's most beautiful creatures, called a butterfly! When it breaks out of its chrysalis, it can spread its wings and fly.

I must get out of the way and let my daughters face their struggles, for it will strengthen them. If I struggle for them, they will die. Mother Mary Woodie said, "When we ask God to save our children, we don't know what He will allow to happen in order to bring them to Him." Mothers, do we trust God to take care of our children? He has not given us a spirit of fear or worry. Those negative feelings come from the enemy of our soul. Fear, worry, and doubt can take us to an early grave or a dark place in our mind. We may not escape from such a diabolical place.

I recently read a beautiful story in a Guidepost magazine. It truly confirmed what God told me about my children. The amazing story was written by a grief-stricken mother. She lost her eighteen-year-old son in a horrific car accident. While planning her son's funeral, she came across a picture of butterflies. She put a picture of a monarch butterfly on the cover of the funeral programs. She wanted to believe something beautiful would come out of the ugly, heartbreaking tragedy that took her son away from her.

She became fascinated with the various species of butterflies. Did you know there are thousands of butterfly species on every continent? Wow, that's amazing. They fly during the day and sleep during the night. They are incredible creatures.

The mother said the great English biologist, Alfred Russell Wallace, observed an emperor butterfly struggling to get out of its chrysalis. He wondered what would happen if he tried to help the struggling creature. He took a knife and opened up the chrysalis and said, "When the butterfly emerged, it spread its wings, drooped perceptibly, and died." He took away the butterfly's struggle to come out when it was strong enough to survive!

The grieving mother said God gave her the strength to go on. He gave her wings to fly during such a painful time in her life. Her love for butterflies helped her through her grieving and healing process. When we release our children to God, we must release ourselves from fear, worry, and guilt. We can't get caught up in what we did or didn't do as a parent. I told my daughters that I was not going to operate out of guilt anymore. I will operate out of love, wisdom, and truth. God doesn't get any glory from our guilt! He is glorified when we begin to grow up in Him!

Our children will come forth as beautiful creatures of the Most High. They're being fashioned by the hands of the Master Potter. We must pray for our children as we train them up in the Lord. We must continue to love them when they're difficult to like. When we stay out of the way as they are growing up in the Lord, He will take good care of them. We don't want them to fall into the traps of the enemy. He hates us and he hates our children. We must not fail to release them into the hands of God. He loves them with an everlasting love!

Where is it, Daddy?

I love the gift of writing! Just as I was flowing with the messages for the first book, I messed up. I misplaced the flash drive on which I had recorded quite a few messages. I then developed the habit of taking it with me for safekeeping. Why didn't I pray for God to keep the contents of my apartment safe? I couldn't find it anywhere. I looked in all of my purses – no flash drive. I panicked after I realized I had failed to save the messages on the hard drive. How was I going to pull up something that doesn't exist? All right, it was time to ask my daddy what happened to the flash drive.

I had a dream that I found the flash drive, but when I woke up I couldn't remember where I found it! When I asked God to help me to find it, He didn't make it reappear. Isn't He the one who is able to do exceedingly and abundantly above all that we can ask or think? Yes, He is, so where is my flash drive, Daddy? Excuse me, for I am about to whine for a just a few moments. Okay, read on.

Didn't my daddy care about the hours that were spent writing and rewriting the messages? What about the people who would be helped when they read the messages? Yes, He does care about the things that concern me. Guess what, I just got it; it's not about me. All of the glory and the praise belong to God, not me. I'm not wasting any more time looking for the flash drive. If I must start over, then it is what it is! Since I surrendered the issue of the flash drive to God, my passion for writing has intensified!

I need to stop writing for a moment and save this message on the hard drive and new flash drives. I bought two of them. I feel so much better; I feel like going on. The unusual calling on my life has completely taken me out of my comfort zone. I invite you to laugh, cry, and grow up with me in the Lord. The Bible says that we can cast our cares on Him because He cares for us. I'm casting all of the issues of my life on Him. I'm going to bed. Goodnight.

I'm About to Give Birth!

This message is about to take you where I didn't want you to go. Now that I've got your attention, I'm about to share what other women don't want to talk about. My doctor performed a medical procedure which would ensure so-called Mother Nature wouldn't make any more frequent and painful visits. Her visits were about to be cut off, snip by snip. My doctor said if I chose to have the surgery I wouldn't be able to have any more children. I gave him a "so what?" look. He told the nurse to schedule my surgery as soon as possible. I was an angry 35-year-old single mother, who wasn't in the mood for any more suffering. Now that I've shared too much, there's no point in withholding the good stuff.

Let me tell you about the slick man who crept into my life when I was about 52 years old. When he came into my life, I had been celibate for over 15 years. He said all of the things that I wanted to hear; trust me, he played his role well. He assured me that he would be there for me through thick and thin. Yeah right, Mister thinned out before things started to get thick! I'm not blaming him for the head games and the bed games we played. I'm setting myself up to be judged. I give you permission to judge me; I'm okay with that. I'm exposing the sin I found in myself. I've spent the majority of my life worrying about what people said or thought about me. God has set me free from focusing on how people may or may not receive me!

Let me ease the mind of the man who wasn't God's choice for me. The sin we committed didn't impregnate me. This is a different type of pregnancy. When I was pregnant with both of my daughters, I couldn't see what the ultra-sound tech tried to show me on the screen. God blessed me with two of the most beautiful, unique daughters. I didn't know we would need each other so much. They are the best part of the relationship I had with their fathers. Will there be a message about the ex boyfriend and the ex husband? I don't think so. I can't put both of the exes in the same message.

When I was growing up, my grandmother Estella used to say things that didn't make sense to me at the time. She used to talk about 'fass' girls. They allowed boys to mess with them until they got pregnant. At the time, I didn't understand what 'mess with them' meant. I lived in fear of a boy getting me pregnant. My grandmother told me if I got pregnant, she wouldn't love me anymore. She never talked to me about sex though, or how a girl or a woman got pregnant. I was left to figure out what she didn't teach me. Here's one of her quotes: "What's done in the dark will come to light." She used this quote when she talked about 'fass' girls. Whenever a girl or a woman becomes pregnant, her swollen belly revealed what was done in the dark. Why aren't there any outward signs to identify the boy or the man who got them pregnant? When the news of the pregnancy was revealed, would the sperm donor man-up or creep into the darkness?

When I got pregnant with my first daughter, my grandmother said she had a dream about fishes. She claimed the dream meant someone close to her was pregnant. Whatever, I wasn't in the mood to hear about her dreams. I couldn't believe she had the nerve to ask me if I was pregnant! Her dipping into my business struck a nerve, so I lied to her. The lie started to swell like my swollen belly, hips, and feet. Trying to hide my pregnancy was like trying to hide an elephant under a rug.

I was 23-years-old when I got pregnant, and I was living on my own. That didn't stop my grandmother from getting on my nerves. After my first beautiful daughter, Brandy Grace Monique, was born, I went to visit my guardians. I became invisible when they saw my daughter. My grandmother and my Aunt Barbara treated Brandy as if she was their baby, not mine.

When the nurse congratulated me on my second pregnancy, I just looked at her. I wish I could tell you I enjoyed my pregnancies. I didn't, and I allowed myself to be treated badly. Here's a quote you may freely use:

"We train people how to treat us." God has empowered me through that quote He gave me. I constantly reminded the fathers of both of my daughters that I regretted the day I got involved with them. On a pain scale of one to ten, in my mind, the pain they gave me deserved a twenty. They deserved double for the pain and the trouble they caused me! I angrily asked God why these men came into my life, and then left me alone to raise my beautiful daughters. He began to show me how fragmented people attract other fragmented people. As a whole woman, I'm no longer interested in a fragmented man. I don't attract them and they're not attracted to me! God is so good to me!

Before I moved from Cleveland, Bishop Kinkaid spoke words of prophecy into my life when I attended a service at Mt. Sinai Baptist Church. When he began to pray for me, he stopped and exclaimed, "God is about to birth something in you that has been lying dormant!" I quickly repented and received the words of prophecy. I went home and dug out the messages I had stopped working on. I sorted them out and began to read them. God ministered to me through the messages. I had lost my hope when I got caught up in a sin trap. My flesh and the spirit of conviction had been at war. I thank God for setting me free. I'm ready to tell you about my unique pregnancy!

I'm "pregnant" with the promise all is well with my soul. I can win any battle that comes my way by keeping my mind on God.

I'm pregnant" with the hope that someone will see how much God loves him or her! He is always just one prayer away.

I'm "pregnant" with the promise that God will never leave me, no matter what! I have never felt safe in the arms of anyone until I rested in His arms.

My pregnancy won't cause my body to expand. There won't be any unusual late night cravings. The news of my pregnancy won't be shared with my former partner in sin!

A totally transformed Pam is walking the steps God has ordered for me. I was born over 55-years ago.

My birth mother Helen was involved with a married man when she became pregnant with me. There was no fanfare to declare my unwanted arrival. Please bear with me; when I read the last sentence it tore me up. The tears are falling so fast. As I was struggling to birth this part of this message, I heard God say, "Just write it the way you feel it. It will help someone!"

Listen, I just got to the core of my anger. My lack of self-worth convinced me I was justified in judging my mother and my father. I was wrong! I'm not writing this to bash them; I'm writing this to set myself free. I must forgive my parents and myself and move on. I no longer feel unwanted or invisible! My parents aren't here to witness my transformation. I'm so proud to announce the birth of a gifted, kindhearted, beautiful, empowered woman. She has accepted her legitimate place as a child of the Most High. Ms. Pam, you are truly somebody! Go ahead, Lady, and encourage yourself in the Lord.

God used someone dear to my heart to speak life-changing words into my life. She's a wonderful servant of God. Her inner beauty compliments her outer beauty. She's highly anointed; she is favored by God. Evangelist Sharon Blevins teaches and preaches with power and authority. God told her to tell me, "The worst is over; the best is yet to come." I cried as I received what was spoken into my life. This message has changed the course of my journey. I hope you will see yourself as God sees you! Birthing this has totally worn me out. I really need to rest!

Chapter 6

It's a Wrap!

Stir it Up!

I'm not a grill master, so my attempt to barbeque wasn't going well. The chicken on the grill still wasn't cooked well enough. The retired chef who taught our culinary art class said, "A case of salmonella can kill you." I removed the chicken from the grill. As I stirred up the coals, they began to heat up. The under-cooked chicken was placed back on the grill until it was done. If I had not taken the time to stir up the coals, the chicken would not have cooked properly. The coals on the bottom were hot; they just needed to be stirred up!

Is it possible to stir up the gifts God has given us? If our dreams appear to be lying dormant within us, can they be stirred up? What can we do if the goals we set haven't been met? Can we stir up the embers of hope within us so our faith doesn't die? Throughout these messages, you will be asked questions which will make you think, and that's good for the mind! Here's some more food for the brain. Why do people waste time whining about their life instead of enjoying it? I'm about to tell you about someone who lived a life of limits and regrets.

As my grandmother, sister, and I stood in the ICU room, I saw pain and regret on my mother's face. Her life was being smoldered out, one labored breath at a time. It was too late for her to dream any more dreams. There would be no more sunrises or sunsets for her to see. There would be no more loud or soft laughter, no more hugs or stolen kisses from lovers who didn't love or respect her. While I was standing by my mother's bed, I saw three generations of women in the ICU room.

The death angel crept in and took one generation into her final destination. The monitor told us what we didn't want to know. The embers of my mother's life had burned out. She spent the majority of her life in pain. She tried to drown out her pain with men, weed, and alcohol. You heard me right. Momma Helen smoked weed! I watched her live a life of regret. She was tormented with spirits of depression and misery. She died a painful death. I don't know if she got right with God; I hope and pray that she did.

We must not let our faith, hope, or dreams smolder until they're dead! I no longer say, "If I knew then what I know now, I would have done things differently." My then and now knowledge is molding me into who I need to be! The things God has spoken into my life will come to pass!

Have you heard the saying, "Misery loves company?" That's not a lie. The spirit of misery is from the Father of lies. Miserable people are more than willing to share their spirits of misery. If we open ourselves up to negative spirits, they won't smolder and die out within us. As long as there is breath in our bodies, we must fight the good fight. When we face difficult seasons, we must hold onto the word of God; weeping may endure for a night, but joy will come in the morning. I hope this message has stirred up a fresh, burning fire within you. If the fire within you has begun to die down, allow your faith to stir it up!

May I Have This Dance?

Hi, Daddy. It's just like you to drop some rich nuggets into my spirit. I reflected back to when I used to go barhopping, now called clubbing. If you wanted to play the barhopping game, you had to look good and smell good. You had to give both your haters and your admirers something to talk about. When I got my high on, it was time to dance. If you looked as good as I did, someone was going to ask you to dance. Whenever my girls and I stepped out, it was ladies' night. We took turns scanning the crowd for potential dance partners. Now, the men were tall, short, light, or dark, and fine as smooth-tasting wine. As a fine, six-foot woman, I preferred the tall, dark, and easy-on-the-eyes gentlemen.

My girls and I enjoyed our evening out until Mr. "Bug-a-boo" arrived. This is the man I tried to pray away! Why was this man in my face? Where did he come from, and what will it take to make him go away? When he asked me to dance, I tried to come up with a lie to shut him down. The lie didn't shut him down *or* shut him up. He kept throwing out lines as foul as his breath. What a waste of some good weed. He just killed my high with his raggedy game.

Oh yeah, listen, the deejay is playing my jam, but I'm not about to dance a slow or fast dance with Mr. "Bug-a-boo." I closed my eyes and prayed he would be gone when I opened them. When I opened my big beautiful eyes, ugh, he was still there. Really, God, you're not going to make him disappear? He just posted himself in front of my wonderful view. I wanted to tell him to get out of my face. I'd better not! What if my rejection causes him to snap? If he takes a trip over the edge, he may take me with him. I came out with my girlfriends to have fun, not to die.

My refusal to talk to him or dance with him doesn't seem to bother him. He seems oblivious to the fine men who are working overtime to get my attention. My salty attitude won't let me enjoy the sweet, sultry music. While Mr. "Bug-a-boo" was running his mouth, Mr. "Fine-as-wine" decided to dance with someone else. I couldn't take it anymore! It was time for my girls and me to go. We just wanted to dance and have fun.

If the men took too long to ask us to dance, we danced with each other. The men would join us on the dance floor or stand around and enjoy the view. Let me stop for a moment and make something very clear! My friends and I weren't looking for anyone who wanted to play head or bed games. We went out to dance and escape from our own personal challenges. When the last call for alcohol was announced, it was time to leave the bar. When my girls and I left the bar, the tall, short, fine-as-wine men were left behind!

Let me backtrack to my former high school days. My need to fit in where I didn't fit in caused me horrific heartbreak. I attended a party that ruined my clean reputation. My cousin Stanley and I attended the same high school. He was a talented, popular senior. He was part of the cool crowd. I was a gullible, needy freshman who just wanted to be accepted. When

Stanley invited me to a party his friends were hosting, I was so excited! I was about to fit in with the popular club. The cost to fit in with the popular crowd, though, came with a high price!

I wore a light blue, see-through blouse with a pretty matching bra, and a pair of thirty-six-inch hip hugging, bell-bottom pants. My Aunt Betty had bought them for me. I no longer wear anything that reveals too much. Any clothing item that may hug my expanded hips too much will be put up until further notice. Sorry, I got off track for a moment! Let me take you to the party, which tarnished my clean reputation.

When Stanley and I arrived at the party, people were dancing or standing around the walls of the basement. Most of the music that was being played was slow. I wanted to fit in, so I danced with any of the guys who asked me to dance. My innocent world was about to get rocked. When I went back to school on Monday, someone had started an ugly rumor about someone who had "the nasty disease." I was horrified when I found out the rumors were about me. If dancing with anyone in a dark or well-lit area would cause me to get "the nasty disease," I will never dance again.

I couldn't believe how I was being treated. I became invisible to the guys I danced with at the party. How could I defend myself? Would anyone believe that I wasn't sexually active? The lies that had been spread about me took a heavy toll. No one but God and I knew about the tears I cried in my secret closet of shame. Stanley knew the truth, but he couldn't stop the rumors. The people who spread the rumors weren't interested in the truth. If they knew the real me, not the Pam I let them to see, would it have stopped them from spreading filthy rumors about me? I'll never know the answer to that question!

I put a smile on my face to cover up my pain. My reputation wasn't ruined because of what I did; people who judged me ruined it. My need to be popular came with a huge price. Being known as the "slut" with "the nasty disease" made me real popular – how sad! The outfit I wore to the party caused me to be judged. Wait a minute. Some of the young ladies at the party wore outfits similar to mine. I don't know why I became the target of the haters.

Ladies, we must use wisdom in the way we dress and carry ourselves. If we reveal too much, we may end up in a bad situation with a terrible reputation that can't be covered up! Bishop T.D Jakes said, "Men wonder if a woman is willing to share what she is willing to show." What are we going to do with the information he gave us? I shared it with you. Pass it on it to other women, for it may bless and educate them!

I'm taking a giant leap from 1967 to 2001. I found a job working as a resident advisor. I was an overseer for a challenging group of ladies and their children. A formal dance had been planned for the young ladies and their escorts. We took our time preparing for the dance and we looked great. I was scheduled to work as the chaperone for the evening. I positioned myself by the front door so I could keep my eyes on what was going on.

As I was monitoring my ladies and their escorts, an uninvited man showed up and asked me to dance. When I politely told him no, he refused to accept my answer. My lifestyle had completely changed, so how did Mr. "I'm-about-to-get-on-your-nerves" creep his way into a wonderful evening? He just stood there and ran his mouth. I gave him the "get out of my face" look. He ignored the look. I tried to ignore him as the old school music was playing.

I chose not to dance to the music of my past! When I turned him down again, he snapped and said, "You don't know how to dance." My flesh said to show him you can dance or tell him off. You can repent later! The devil is a liar; it was time to pray him away. God is certainly my refuge and strength and a very present help in trouble. I hid in Him so I didn't get into trouble. Mr. "Getting-on-my-nerves" is about to get checked. My supervisor came over and asked him who had invited him to the dance. After he mumbled his answer, he was asked to leave.

God quickly took care of the situation for me. My choice of music and the way I dance has changed. My dance partner is a gentleman. He would never force himself on me. He's there with me even when I don't feel like dancing. The sweet melodies of our hearts may cause us to dance when no one can hear the music. If you're unable to dance, just let the melodies of your heart dance for you. I'm about to dance on some toes.

The enemy of our soul has crept into our praise and worship services. It's time to get real when our young people say, "Some Christian music and videos have gone too far!" My daughters told me about something that happened while they were at a club. While they were on the dance floor, the deejay played a gospel song. All of the young people who were brought up in church got off the dance floor. They didn't return to the dance floor until the deejay played a non-gospel song. Dance in your heart if you can't dance with your body. Enjoy the melodies of your heart and dance on! Excuse me; my dance partner is waiting for me. It's time for us to dance. The lady in me won't keep my gentleman waiting too long!

It's Time to Go Back Home!

God recently blessed me to move into a beautiful, senior citizen apartment building. My apartment is amazing! He gave me what I asked for. Give me a moment to boast about the goodness of the Lord. I had recently been evicted from the apartment in Cleveland. I had lived there for about eight years. Would you like to know why I got evicted? Okay, read on.

I made foolish choices that started the eviction drama. When I stood before the judge in eviction court, I was in tears. My property manager told the judge she was willing to work with me. She had been my former supervisor and we had become good friends, but our friendship was about to be tested. She worked out a payment plan for me, which looked good on paper. When the agency that assured me of their help backed out, I wasn't able to keep the payment arrangement. My friends and loved ones tried to help me, but I was behind in everything. A green eviction tag was posted on the outside of our building. I called the manager to tell her about the tag. She said it was probably a mistake. I ignored the warning and went to work.

As I was doing my chores, my daughter Brandy called to tell me my stuff was being put out on the street. She and my grandchildren lived in the building across from me. The reality of what she said sunk in fast. A friend of mine showed up at my daughter's place of work to tell her about the eviction. He told her to get in touch with me as soon as possible. When Brandy told her boss what was going on, he told her to leave to check on me. I tried to calm down as I was talking to my boss about the eviction. Once I started crying, the tears wouldn't stop falling. I tried to wrap my mind around what was happening at my former residence.

I called the man with whom I had enjoyed our seasons of sin. He said he would be there for me. I fell apart when I was talking to him; I couldn't hide the pain I was feeling. Before I parked on the street, I saw a crowd gathered by my things. I walked in a daze towards the building, which I would never call home again.

My friend Orlando walked up to me and let me fall into his large, strong arms and cry. The shock and pain were too much! Would I make it through this ordeal? Orlando reminded me that I had always been there for him and other people. He said, "Miss Pam, it's time for you to be encouraged, not judged." His words of encouragement would come back to me later. My heart felt as if it was going to stop beating at any moment!

I tried to convince myself everything was going to be all right. As Brandy and my closest friends rallied around me, other people I barely knew came to my rescue! Everyone was working hard to put my things in my daughter's apartment. God used them to help me as I still walked around in a daze. The men that were putting my things out thought I knew about the eviction. They apologized to my daughter for doing what they had to do. I kept telling myself, *it wasn't supposed to end like this!*

I looked at the bed I shared with a man who said that he loved me. Where was he? He said that he would be here for me. Why wasn't he here to console me? I wanted to hear him say, "I love you, Baby; it's going to be alright. Was he ashamed to be seen with me, or was it my imagination? Yeah, right! I didn't imagine the eviction. I had to face the truth–he lied to me. He never intended to be there for me. Do you think he ever missed an opportunity to commit sin with me? I can assure you he found the time to stop by to get what he wanted! I believe he did a drive-by, and then chose not to stop by to see about me. He already got what he wanted; he didn't want to deal with my problems or me. I got his message loud and clear. I shifted my focus back to all of the people who really were there for me!

As I was dealing with the shock of the eviction, my mind went back to the property manager. I needed to call her and tell her off. In my mind, I had nothing to lose. As soon as I heard her voice, I flipped on her. When I allowed her to speak, the conversation got real ugly. She didn't want to deal with my eviction issue or me. I hung up on her while she was still talking, I told her off; *mission accomplished.*

My daughter stored my things in her apartment. I wandered from place to place. I slept in my truck when I didn't want to be around anyone. God kept me safe during the most painful time of my life. I continued to work until I took a bad fall one night after leaving my job. My truck was parked in an area that was as dark as my life had become. The fall I took at my job wasn't my fault, but the fall I took during my season of sin was!

When God gave me another chance to repent, I ran into His arms. He assured me His love for me is unconditional. I refuse to fall back into the arms of the man who lusted for me. I gave him what he didn't deserve. We can accept the truth or we can reject it. I chose to accept it! Do any of you remember the lyrics of the song, "Everybody plays the fool?" I'm no longer playing the role of a fool! God delivered me out of my sin trap before it was too late. Am I going to reap what I have sown? Yes, I am. I won't rest in the arms of another man who doesn't love me or respect me. If you're not willing to man up, and husband up, you clearly are not who God has for me.

I had no intentions of moving back to Akron. When my truck was stolen for the second time within a month, I knew that it was time to go! When I moved back home, I lived from place to place. My sweet social worker, Sheila, found a space for me at a real nice shelter. The majority of the people in the house didn't speak English, but we learned how to communicate with one another. I learned to be patient as we shared the bathrooms, the kitchen, and the washer and dryer.

I learned how to shut my mouth to keep peace in the house. I had to remind myself we were all at the shelter for an appointed time. Most of us tried to make the best of our living arrangements. I left for a couple of days to take a break from my roommate. When I walked into the bedroom door, a strong odor of alcohol greeted me! My roommate was lying partially on the floor and her bed. When she looked up and saw me, she flipped out. In her drunken state of mind, she said what she wasn't brave enough to say when she was sober. Grandmother Estella said, "A drunk mind speaks sober thoughts." You're right, Grandma!

When my drunken roommate started to cuss at me, I asked her who she was talking to. She and the demons in her assured me they were talking to me. My roommate was angry because the nun that ran the shelter asked her about about my stolen processions. The woman said, "I didn't steal any money out of your purse." My purse was never left out in the open. It was hidden in the bottom of the closet. She said, "I didn't steal your food. Someone else stole it." I'm changing her name to Someone Else Stole It.

Now let me pause for a moment. I need to thank and praise God for being saved! The praise break is over! All right, I'm back to the roommate who needs to shut up and go to sleep! Listen to what the silly woman told me: "I'm going to get up and hit you real hard." I told her what to expect if she got up and hit me real hard! My roommate was pretty drunk, but she wasn't drunk enough to get up to hit me.

When the woman sat up on her bed to face me, she glared at me! When she hissed, "We curse you," that did it. I had taken enough of her and her posse of demons. I spoke to her and the demons inside of her. I assured them they would not curse my blessed life. When I left the bedroom to cool off, the woman got up and locked me out of the bedroom. The resident advisor finally convinced her to unlock the door. I was told to get my bedclothes and spend the night in the basement! I made sure that I grabbed my purse. I was quite salty. Why wasn't the drunken one sent to the basement? Was it because of a safety issue? Her falling down any of the steps before she reached basement could have caused a severe, or even fatal fall. I didn't want anything to happen to her. I wanted her to shut up and leave me alone. God kept me together throughout the roommate standoff.

After I woke up the next morning, I gathered my things together and went back upstairs. When my roommate finally unlocked the door, I was on my cell phone talking about her. I made sure that she heard what I was saying. Let me assure you that I was "wrong as two left shoes" and "two wrongs don't make a right." Save these clichés for what I'm about to tell you.

When the woman turned around and glared at me, I knew she was about to go off on me again. I wasn't in the mood for her or the demons inside of her. I slammed the door in her face and locked it! She stood outside of the locked door and ranted for a while. When she saw that I wasn't about to deal with them, they left me alone. The resident advisor reported the woman's behavior to the nun that ran the shelter. I was told to pack up her belongings so they could be taken to her.

The woman couldn't see how God was using me to be a blessing to her. I didn't mind sharing some of my things with her. I did mind her stealing my money and my good food! I never confronted her about what she did, but I didn't trust her. I did trust the rest of the people in the house. After she left, God blessed me to move into a room I didn't have to share. When I asked about my ex-roommate, I was told she'd left another house to live back on the streets. I didn't rejoice about her homelessness; it bothered me. Her state of mind led her to where she felt safe.

As I was standing in line at a fast-food restaurant, my friend Trent walked in. He was sitting in his girlfriend's car until he saw me. When he introduced me to his girlfriend Beverly, we laughed and talked about the past. When I told them I was homeless, it took a moment for Trent to recover from the shock. He said, "You ought to fill out an application at the building where I live."

I had just been turned down for an apartment. The eviction on my record wasn't exactly a plus to any potential property manager. When I told Miss Larita, the property manager, why I got evicted, she listened to me and didn't judge me. This is what she said: "Miss Pam, all of us have made mistakes. God will work everything out for you." I thank Him for using Trent and Miss Larita to be such a blessing to me.

When I asked God for an apartment, this is what I asked for: 1. It had to be on one floor because of some health concerns. 2. An island in the kitchen. 3. A balcony so I could enjoy the outdoors in peace. 4. It had to be affordable. I couldn't endure another eviction. 5. I wanted to finally feel safe. I trusted God to help me. I refused to believe my dreams wouldn't come true. When Trent called me, and said, "You got the apartment," I loudly praised God in His ear. When I apologized for screaming in his ear, he laughed.

When I went to fill out my paperwork, Miss Larita gave me the key to my apartment. When I opened up the door of my new apartment, I dropped my purse on the floor. I just stood there and looked at the island and the balcony. My apartment was on the fifth floor. When I reminded God about my fear of heights, He said, "I gave you what you needed." I prayed as I opened up the door of the balcony. I stepped out onto the balcony, and as I looked over the side, I had no fear. I just stood there and cried. God answered my prayers. When I heard Him say, "You're safe," I really broke down and cried. Everything I needed was on my floor, including the laundry room–what a bonus.

God you're so incredible! You have always been there for me. My apartment has been transformed into my home for a season. This isn't my final destination. Wherever I am, I can rest in God's peace.

I called my friend/former property manager to apologize to her. I totally blamed her for the chaotic mess I had caused! I was the one who made the foolish choices that turned my life upside-down. When I declared the eviction was a blessing in disguise, it freed her. In my heart, I knew she felt bad about what she had to do. She graciously accepted my apology. When I went to see her, we hugged, laughed, and talked about the changes in our lives. The plans God has for our lives are to prosper us, not to destroy us. Are you homesick? Do you want to go back home? Your loving Father is waiting for you! Please don't keep Him waiting, too long!

About the Author

The author of *No Test, no Testimony,* Pamela Jean Coston, arrived on the scene at 4:34 p.m. on the ninth of August in 1954. In her own words, Ms. Coston states, "My mother Helen wasn't thrilled about my arrival. She didn't know she was carrying greatness in her womb."

"I can't afford to take my role as a child of God, a mother, and a grandmother for granted! I don't have a title, which may or may not impress anyone. I do have an insatiable desire to reach people before it's too late!"

"I began writing in 1998 to express what I couldn't verbalize. When I began to write, I realized the activity was therapeutic for me. I talked to God about writing a book, thinking it might help other women confront the issues of their painful past. He said, 'Women don't have a *monopoly on pain.*' Every message which God has inspired me to write will help someone. I know many of you are hurting, and you want the pain to stop. Whatever you're going through, give it to God. He can do what you can't do for yourself. Other people may fail you, but He won't! Whatever you need is in Him!"

"My prayer is that someone will choose to live and not die! My prayer is that someone will see his or her true value! My prayer is that someone will find a reason to hold on when they feel like giving up! My prayer is that God will snatch someone out of whatever sin trap in which they're caught. My prayer is that someone will repent and accept Jesus Christ as their personal Savior, before it's too late."

"I will not apologize for the contents of the messages. They were not written to offend anyone. They were written to encourage you and to challenge you to become who you're ordained to be in the Lord. It doesn't matter what you think of me. It's not about me. It's all about the Lord! That's all I have to say!"

www.ingramcontent.com/pod-product-compliance
Lightning Source LLC
LaVergne TN
LVHW051236080426
835513LV00016B/1618